FIGURE SKATING

SHARPEN YOUR SKILLS
Indiana/World Skating Academy

796.912
FIG

MASTERS PRESS

A Division of Howard W. Sams & Co.

Published by Masters Press (A division of Howard W. Sams & Co.)
2647 Waterfront Pkwy. E. Dr., Suite 300
Indianapolis, IN 46214

MD

Published 1995
Printed in the United States of America

Library of Congress Cataloging-in-Publication Data

Figure skating : sharpen your skills / Indiana/World Skating Academy ;
    edited by Patricia Hagen.
        p.   cm. — (Spalding Sports Library)
    At head of title: Spalding
    ISBN 1-57028-007-X : $12.95
    1. Figure Skating.   I. Hagen, Patty, 1959-   .   II. Indiana/World
SkatingAcademy.   III. Title: Spalding figure skating : sharpen your skills.
IV. Series.
GV850.4.F54   1994   94-43117
796.9'12--dc20   CIP

Acknowledgments:

USFSA dance diagrams reprinted with permission by the USFSA

Edited by Patricia Hagen

Cover design: Julie Biddle and Suzanne Lincoln

In-house Editor: Heather Seal

Proofreader: Kathy Prata

Assistance provided by Terry Varvel.

Table of Contents

About the Authors

Figure Skating: Sharpen Your Skills was written by professional coaches who teach at the Indiana/World Skating Academy in Indianapolis, Indiana, and other skating facilities.

JENNIFER CASHEN has been a skating instructor since 1989 in the Indianapolis area. She has directed the learn-to-skate program of the Sycamore Ice Skating Club and is on the staff of I/WSA. Her students have included state champions and regional and sectional competitors. She is a member of the Professional Skaters Guild of America and the United States Figure Skating Association. She passed the USFSA seventh figure, novice free skating and silver dance tests. She is a volunteer instructor in Special Olympics.

SUSAN PITTMAN CLARK has taught learn-to-skate classes and private lessons since 1986 at I/WSA and other arenas. She has trained beginners as well as regional and sectional competitors. She also has worked with skaters at many training camps and seminars. She is a member of the PSGA and USFSA. She earned USFSA gold medals in figures and freestyle and passed the silver dance and bronze pair tests. She is a volunteer instructor for Special Olympics.

PATRICIA HAGEN has coached since 1987 in Indianapolis. She is an instructor in the I/WSA learn-to-skate program and also teaches private lessons. A member of the PSGA, she holds certified ratings in dance and group instruction. She earned a USFSA gold medal in dance and has served on the USFSA Adult Skaters Advisory Committee. She performed in Disney on Ice shows in the United States, the Far East and Australia. She is also a journalist.

PIETER KOLLEN has spent his 30-year coaching career at the Cleveland Skating Club, Broadmoor Skating Club and Indiana/World Skating Academy. He has coached figure skaters at all levels from beginners through Olympians. He also has coached hockey teams and taught power skating to mites through professional hockey players. He is the director of figure skating at I/WSA. A PSGA board member for 15 years, he holds master ratings in figures and free skating, pairs and group instruction. He is a USFSA gold medalist in figures and freestyle, pairs and dance. He was the national champion in pairs and silver medalist in dance in 1962, and a member of the U.S. World Team two years. He also competed as a professional. He has been active on the USFSA Sports Medicine, Music and Competition committees.

SANDY LAMB has been a skating instructor for 27 years in Indianapolis and other cities. She has coached skaters at all levels, including beginners, national champions and Olympians. A past president of the PSGA, she is master rated in group instruction, dance and free dance, and program direction. She is a judge and referee at professional skating competitions. She earned USFSA and Canadian gold medals in dance and a U.S. gold medal in free dance. She competed at the national level in dance and was an alternate to the U.S. World Team in 1966. She is the Indiana State Special Olympics figure skating director and national figure skating director for Special Olympics International. She has coached at three International Winter Special Olympics Games.

KELLEY MORRIS has been coaching skaters since 1981 in Indianapolis and other cities. Her students have included beginners and national champions. She is the director of the I/WSA learn-to-skate program and co-director of the dance program. She holds a PSGA master rating in dance and free dance and a registered rating in figures and free skating. She earned a USFSA gold medal in dance and passed the International Dance Test. She was the U.S. Silver Dance champion in 1977 and has also won medals in international professsional competitions. She was a soloist, choreographer, assistant producer and director for Magic Harbor Parks ice shows in Myrtle Beach, S.C. She has served on the USFSA Basic Skills Committee.

Contributor:
BRIAN WRIGHT has been a choreographer and skating coach since 1989. Artistic director at I/WSA for three years, he works in skating clubs across the country. Selected as Choreographer of the Year in 1994 by the PSGA and USFSA, he has choreographed routines for national champions, Olympians and top professional skaters. He has choreographed shows for Ice Capades and performed in professional ice shows. He is also a professional actor and dancer.

Thanks to the following skaters who were photographed for this book: Donald Adair, Matthew Kessinger, Robyn Lane, Kelley Morris and Dana Podlejski.

Photos by Susan Plageman.

Diagrams by Julie Biddle and Kelli Ternet.

Chapter 1
Introduction to Skating

Welcome to figure skating. You've chosen a sport that offers something for everyone, regardless of their age, physical talents or goals.

Figure skating is a unique combination of athleticism and artistry. It is a sport that will demand your physical and creative energy. In return, skating will give you enjoyment and exercise for a lifetime.

This book will help you get a good, safe start in figure skating, whether your goal is to be a recreational skater or an Olympic champion.

The first two chapters answer many questions commonly asked by people beginning to figure skate. You will learn about the organization of the sport, lessons, and equipment.

The basics chapter includes easy-to-follow instructions for taking your first steps and doing many basic maneuvers. When you have mastered those skills, you're ready for the chapters on figures, free skating (also known as freestyle) and ice dancing, three of the disciplines of figure skating. Each of these chapters provides an introduction to the discipline — start with the one that interests you most and then try the others.

Pair skating, the fourth discipline of figure skating, is not covered in this book. Skaters who are interested in pair skating should first learn the jumps and spins discussed in the free skating chapter.

In each chapter, the skills are presented in order from the easiest to the most difficult. It's important that you work through the skills in order. You can easily keep track of your progress by using the checklist at the end of each chapter. When you master a skill, check it off and move on to the next, more difficult skill.

Authors
The instructions and advice in this book are tried and true methods used by the experienced professional coaches who teach at Indiana/World Skating Academy and Research Center in Indianapolis, Indiana.

Since the two-rink facility opened in 1987, thousands of skaters have learned and polished their skills here. The academy operates a year-round learn-to-skate program and offers training programs for local and international competitors.

The coaches who contributed to this book have more than 100 combined years of experience teaching skaters of all ages in all facets of figure skating.

QUESTIONS AND ANSWERS

As you get started in figure skating, you will have many questions about the sport. Here are answers to some common questions:

1. HOW DO I GET STARTED?

First, locate an ice rink. Facilities in your area are listed in the yellow pages of your telephone book. Also, call your local parks and recreation department and inquire about rinks and programs. Indoor facilities offer year-round skating in many communities.

Most rinks schedule public-skating sessions, when you may skate for a nominal fee. Most rinks also rent skates. At the rink, you can inquire about learn-to-skate group lessons and private instruction.

You will need to buy or rent figure skates. For some advice on equipment, see page 11 (Equipment Chapter).

2. SHOULD I TAKE CLASSES?

Yes, if you are interested in a fun, social, relatively inexpensive way to learn to skate or improve your skills. Most skaters take group lessons at the start of their skating careers. Some skaters take classes at advanced levels. Skating classes are offered even for tiny tots, starting at about age 3.

Classes generally follow one of two popular learn-to-skate programs: the United States Figure Skating Associations' Basic Skills Program or the Ice Skating Institute of America's Recreational Ice Skater Test Program. Many rinks, however, develop their own learn-to-skate programs.

Both the USFSA and ISIA programs are standardized for use at rinks nationwide. Both offer instruction for all ages and skill levels, from beginning through advanced. In both programs, skaters are rewarded with patches when they master specific skills.

3. WHAT IS THE USFSA?

The United States Figure Skating Association is commonly referred to as the USFSA. It is the national governing body of figure skating.

A skater may join the association by paying dues as an individual member or by joining a member club. The USFSA has grown to 120,000 registered skaters since it was formed in 1921. Your local skating rink may be the home base of a USFSA member club.

The *Rulebook* of the USFSA contains rules of the sport, explanations of figures, freestyle, pairs and dances, the test structure and related information.

In learn-to-skate programs that follow the USFSA Basic Skills Program, skaters may take tests and earn awards in basic figure skating skills, figures, freestyle, dance, power skating and precision.

More advanced skaters may take proficiency tests in figures, free skating, pairs and dance. The tests start with basic maneuvers and get progressively more difficult. It is quite an accomplishment to pass the "gold" test in any branch of the sport.

The USFSA also sanctions competitions for members. Competitions are organized for skaters of all ages and skill levels, including beginners. Basic skills competitions offer beginning skaters an opportunity to perform and compete immediately. The best skaters can work their way up the competitive ladder and qualify for the U.S. Nationals, World Championships and Olympic Winter Games.

USFSA member clubs organize shows in which members can perform. Club membership is a good way to meet other skaters and participate in recreational and training programs.

For more information, contact the USFSA at 20 First Street, Colorado Springs, CO 80906-3697.

4. WHAT IS THE ISIA?

ISIA stands for Ice Skating Institute of America. The institute oversees a recreational skating program for about 112,000 members at more than 400 ice rinks across the country. Your local rink may be a member of the ISIA and offer classes that follow the ISIA's Recreational Ice Skater Test Program. ISIA members from 2 to 75 years old have been participating in the program since the early 1960s.

Skaters can earn awards at 76 test levels, including basic skills, freestyle, figures, ice dancing, pair skating, couple skating, speed skating and hockey.

The ISIA endorses competitions for recreational skaters of all ages at the local and national levels.

For more information, contact the ISIA at 355 West Dundee Road, Buffalo Grove, IL 60089-3500.

5. SHOULD I TAKE PRIVATE LESSONS?

Private lessons are for skaters who want to work one on one with a coach. Semi-private lessons, in which two or three skaters receive instruction from one coach, are a less expensive way to get individualized attention.

Skaters typically begin private lessons when they want extra help on skills taught in classes or because they want to make faster progress than they can in a class or on their own. Whether or not you take private lessons depends on your budget and your goals.

6. HOW MUCH PRACTICE TIME DO I NEED?

As much as possible. You will progress faster if you practice between classes or private lessons. Two or three practice sessions a week will be enough for most beginners.

It's a good idea to arrive at the rink at least a half hour before your lesson so you can warm up and practice. If possible, stay and practice at least a half hour after your lesson.

In addition to public sessions, your rink or skating club may offer sessions for practicing free skating, dance and figures. Generally, you will not receive instruction in these sessions unless you schedule a private lesson with a coach.

7. HOW DO I FIND A COACH?

Your rink may have a staff of coaches, or "pros," that offers private instruction. Some coaches specialize in one aspect of figure skating, such as dance or freestyle. Other instructors teach all the disciplines. Information about coaches may be available through the rink office or the resident skating club. For recommendations, talk to skaters at your rink.

Once you hire a coach, you will schedule private lessons with the coach at a time that's convenient for both of you.

8. WHAT CHARACTERISTICS SHOULD I LOOK FOR IN A PRO?

The student/coach relationship is extremely important to success in skating. You should try to find a qualified coach with whom you can communicate easily.

If possible, take a trial lesson or two from a coach to find out if you like his or her personality and teaching style.

Here are some questions to ask a potential coach:
1. How many years have you been coaching?
2. What is your skating background (tests passed, competitive record, show experience)?
3. Are you a member of the Professional Skaters Guild of America? Have you earned a rating from the PSGA?
4. How much do you charge for a lesson?
5. When are you available for lessons?

9. WHAT IS THE PSGA?

The Professional Skaters Guild of America is the largest organization of ice skating professionals in the world, with 2,200 members. All of the authors of this book are members of the PSGA.

The PSGA has developed a rating system for coaches that is recognized worldwide. A PSGA rating is a credential that some skaters look for when choosing a coach.

A PSGA-rated professional has coaching experience and has been examined by a panel of expert coaches. To earn a rating, a coach must demonstrate knowledge in a particular area of skating: figures and freestyle, dance, pairs, group instruction, program administration, precision team instruction, choreography and style, and power stroking. Ratings are given at the registered, certified, senior and master levels of proficiency.

10. HOW MUCH DO PRIVATE LESSONS COST?

Coaching fees vary widely. Rates range from $10 to more than $50 per half hour, depending on the coach's credentials and experience. Rates generally are higher in large cities and on the East and West coasts. Some coaches will teach semi-private lessons in which two or three skaters split the cost.

Lessons may last from 15 minutes to an hour depending on the skater's and coach's schedules. Some skaters take private lessons occasionally, others take several a day.

11. WHAT EXERCISES CAN I DO OFF THE ICE TO IMPROVE MY SKATING?

Skaters need to be strong and flexible. Some skaters build their strength with a carefully planned weight-training program. Stretching exercises are used to increase flexibility.

Aerobic exercise, such as aerobic dancing or riding a stationary bicycle, can help a skater improve endurance.

Many of the best figure skaters take ballet or other dance classes. Dance is good for a skater who wants to work on posture, flexibility, strength and musical interpretation. Some rinks and skating clubs organize dance classes that are designed specifically for skaters.

12. HOW SHOULD I WARM UP AT THE START OF A PRACTICE SESSION?

Cold bodies are more likely to get injured, so warming up is essential to safe skating. You should stretch and do other warm-up exercise before getting on the ice.

On the ice, start with stroking, edges and crossovers (discussed in the basics chapter) to get your body moving. Slowly work up to faster and more difficult moves.

After you have skated for several minutes to warm up, do some stretching exercises on the ice.

13. WHAT CAN I DO TO PROTECT MYSELF FROM INJURY?

Do stretching and warm-up exercises before skating strenuously.

Learn to stop as soon as possible. Learn to fall correctly and get up quickly.

Keep your equipment in good repair.

Make sure you lace your skates correctly. Use a double knot at the top and make sure the lace loops are not hanging where they can be snagged with the other skate.

Wear appropriate clothing. Avoid loose pants that could be snagged by your skates. Beginning skaters should wear gloves and a hat for extra padding in case of a fall.

Don't wear a headset while skating. You won't be as aware of the people around you on the ice.

Look where you are going. Frequently check behind you when practicing backward moves. Don't get so caught up in what you are practicing that you don't see other people.

Don't practice advanced skills during crowded public sessions.

14. HOW CAN I PROTECT MY CHILD AT THE RINK?
Supervise your child carefully, especially during crowded public sessions.

Make sure your child's skates fit and are laced correctly.

Make sure your child learns to skate safely and correctly.

Children should be taught how to fall down safely and get up quickly. Your child can be enrolled in group lessons when he or she is about 3 years old. (Your rink may have a minimum age requirement.)

Dress the child appropriately. Mittens are always a good idea. A hat may soften bumps if the child falls; some children wear hockey helmets. Snowpants will help keep the child dry.

Do not carry your child in your arms while on the ice.

Do not walk on the ice in your street shoes while helping a child. You may slip and injure yourself.

Chapter 2
Equipment

A figure skater needs only a few pieces of equipment, the most important of which are the skates. Figure skates consist of a boot, preferably made of leather, and steel blades.

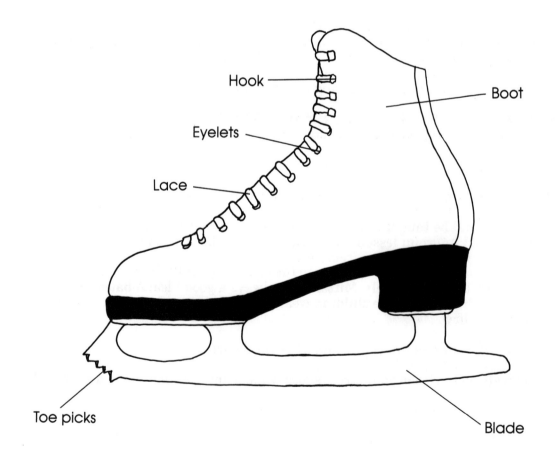

Hook

Boot

Eyelets

Lace

Toe picks

Blade

Figure skates differ from hockey and speed skates in movement and appearance. Figure skating boots look like high-top shoes with heels. Hockey and speed skating boots are lower cut and do not have heels.

Figure skating blades are distinguished by the toe picks — the row of teeth at the front. The toe picks are used for jumping and spinning, not for stopping. Hockey blades are shorter and more curved from front to back. Speed skating blades are longer than hockey or figure blades; the length allows a speed skater to move faster.

Some advanced skaters use different pairs of skates for doing figures, free skating and ice dancing because the blades are designed differently for each specialty. People who are beginning to learn to skate only need one pair of general-purpose skates.

In addition to a pair of skates, skaters may find some accessories are helpful:

If you own rather than rent skates, be sure to buy a pair of blade guards. Made of plastic or rubber, guards will protect your blades from nicks and scratches and help them remain sharp longer. Always put guards on your blades when you wear skates off the ice. Do not store your skates with the guards on the blades. Terry cloth blade covers can be used to protect the blades when skates are not being worn.

A skate bag is helpful for carrying your skates and other accessories to and from the rink. A bag will protect your equipment and keep it all in one place. The pro shop at your rink may sell bags specifically designed for carrying skates, but a small suitcase or athletic bag will suffice.

Wear clothes that keep you warm and allow you to move comfortably. Keep gloves or mittens and an extra sweater in your skate bag in case you get chilled.

Keep an extra set of laces in your skate bag in case you break one.

A USFSA *Rulebook* is a handy guide to the sport, especially for skaters who take USFSA tests or participate in competitions. The *Rulebook* contains official rules for tests and competitions, and diagrams for figures and ice dances. The *ISIA Skaters and Coaches Handbook* includes standards for ISIA tests, and other information.

Some skaters who practice figures use a scribe, a device that works like a compass, to draw circles on the ice.

Lacing your skates
Before learning to skate, every skater should learn to lace their skates correctly. Lacing may be time-consuming at first, but, with practice, you will get faster.

Here's the procedure:

1. Loosen the laces. Pull the tongue up and forward.
2. Insert your foot, fitting your heel snugly in the back of the boot. Tuck in the tongue.
3. Starting at the toe, pull the laces tightly. Use both hands. The laces should be tightest around your ankle.
4. Work your way up the hooks, crossing the laces and wrapping them around each pair of hooks. Make sure the laces aren't too tight at the top hooks ... you have to be able to bend your ankle.
5. At the top, tie the laces in a bow and double knot it.
6. Tuck the ends of the laces and the loops between the laces and the tongue.

1

2

3

4

5

6

Lacing tips

If the laces are too long, get shorter laces. Do not wrap the laces around and around the top of the skate.

It is both sloppy and dangerous to let long loops dangle from the bow. You might snag a loop with your other skate and fall.

QUESTIONS AND ANSWERS

Here are some answers to questions beginning skaters often ask about skates and other skating equipment.

1. SHOULD I BUY OR RENT SKATES?

That depends on your skill level and the availability and quality of rental skates. If your rink rents skates, try them out to make sure they are adequate. Questions to consider: Are the boots leather? Are they sturdy enough to support your ankles? Do they fit well? Are the blades sharp?

If you are a beginner and decent rental skates are available, don't rush to buy new skates. Wait until you are sure you will stick with the sport.

Small children usually do well in rental skates. Besides, it's too expensive to keep buying skates for feet that keep growing. Generally, rental skates in the smallest sizes are not as worn as the larger sizes; they don't get as much use.

Skaters who plan to take private lessons in addition to group lessons need to have their own skates. The money spent on private lessons will be wasted if you try to practice in poor-quality rentals.

Good skates are a big investment. The skates you buy will depend on your budget and your goals. A pair of new skates, suitable for a recreational skater, costs between $100 and $200. When you have mastered basic jumps and spins, you will probably want and need better skates. Competitive figure skaters spend hundreds of dollars on a set of boots and blades.

Be careful when buying used skates and using hand-me-downs. Used skates can be a way to reduce the cost of equipping yourself, but be sure the skates are in good condition and the correct size. If the skates belonged to your mother years ago, forget it!

2. I HAVE WEAK ANKLES. CAN I BE A SKATER?

Chances are you don't have weak ankles, you have weak skates. Good-quality, sturdy skates don't allow your ankles to bend toward the ice.

Make sure your skates are in good condition and not too old and broken down. Hold one skate by the top of the ankle. Turn it so the bottom of the blade is up. If the boot collapses, falling to either side, the skates are worn out and should be replaced.

Make sure the skates are the correct size. Many people wear skates that are too big, offering little support for their feet and ankles. Hand-me-downs and borrowed skates are seldom the correct size. You may have a painful or even dangerous experience if you wear them.

Also, make sure the skates are laced correctly. Loosely laced skates won't support your ankles.

3. WHERE SHOULD I BUY SKATES?

Buy skates in a reputable pro shop in a skating rink. Pro shops are more likely to have salespeople who have the time and expertise to help you select and fit skates correctly.

Don't waste your money buying skates from department or sporting goods stores. The skates you find in those types of stores usually are of poor quality and the salespeople generally don't know how to fit skates.

Ask your instructor or other skaters where to buy skates in your area.

4. WHAT KIND OF SKATES SHOULD I BUY?

Buy skates with leather boots. Avoid plastic boots.

Avoid skates that have blades riveted to the sole.

Do not buy double-runner skates, even for a small child. Double runners will not allow the child to learn to glide.

A skater learning basic skills can buy an adequate pair of skates off the shelf in a pro shop. These skates cost about $100-$200.

Once you graduate from basic skills, you will probably want to buy your boots and blades separately, choosing brands that suit your needs and budget. There are several companies that manufacture boots and blades that are popular among figure skaters.

Each manufacturer makes a range of stock boots to suit skaters ranging from beginners to world champions. A rule of thumb: The more you spend, the better the skate. More-expensive, better-quality skates are made with more layers of leather for better support. Better skates also have more padding for comfort around the heel and ankle.

The boot manufacturers offer custom-made boots for skaters who want or need them. Unless you have foot problems or an unusual size, custom skates are an unnecessary expense for a beginner.

Talk with your instructor and an expert in the pro shop before buying boots and blades; they may help you avoid making an expensive mistake.

5. HOW DO I KNOW IF MY SKATES FIT CORRECTLY?

A common mistake is renting or buying skates that are too large. Skates that are too big will not properly support your foot and ankle. Generally, your skate size should be at least a size smaller than your shoe size.

The boot should fit snugly — more snugly than street shoes. Your toes should be close to the front of the skate. You should be able to move your toes, but the ball of your foot should not move inside the skate. Your heel should sit snugly in the back of the skate. When your skates are laced correctly, your heel should not slip up and down inside the boot.

When laced, there should be about 2 inches of space between the two lines of eyelets on new skates. The lacing will be narrower as the boots are broken in and the leather stretches.

You have a better chance of getting the correct size if you buy your skates in a pro shop with an experienced salesperson.

6. HOW MANY PAIRS OF SOCKS SHOULD I WEAR?

One pair of thin socks or tights is enough. You don't want thick socks or two layers of socks between your foot and your skate.

When you go to a pro shop to buy skates, wear the socks or tights you plan to wear when you skate.

7. HOW DO I KEEP MY FEET WARM IN THE COLD RINK?

Keep practicing. Your feet will get colder if you stand around. Also, make sure your skates are laced correctly. If laced too tight at the top of the ankle or across the toes, circulation may be constricted.

Leg warmers may help. Knitted warmers can be bunched around your ankle and pulled down around the heel of the skate. It also helps to buy better-quality skates. They have more padding and, therefore, keep your feet warmer. Boot covers, which are available in some pro shops, also will help keep the warmth inside the skate.

8. WHAT SHOULD I DO IF MY SKATES MAKE MY FEET HURT?

Before giving up on skating, check several things:
Make sure your skates are the correct size.
Make sure your socks are not bunched up or creased.
Make sure your skates are laced properly: tight around the ankle, looser around the top of the boot.

New skates usually feel very stiff, and the boot may rub against your ankle or heel. Try to alleviate the pressure before you get a blister. You can prevent or protect sore spots by padding the area with various foot-care products available in drug stores. Experiment with adhesive bandages, tape, "second skin," moleskin or spongy makeup pads. But don't add padding to tight spots. It will only make the spot hurt more.

Sometimes the boot leather can be stretched with a special implement to make more room at the spots that hurt. Talk to your instructor or pro shop.

If you have orthopedic problems, you may need orthotics prescribed by a doctor or custom-made skates.

9. WHAT'S THE BEST WAY TO BREAK IN NEW SKATES?

New skates are beautiful, but very stiff. Breaking them in can be an uncomfortable, even painful, process — but it's worth it. When your feet get warm and sweat, the heat and moisture soften the leather and help it form to your foot.

There are almost as many breaking-in methods as there are skaters. Try one or more of these suggestions:

Skate for a half hour, then take off the new skates and rest your feet for 15 minutes. Repeat. Note: You probably won't be able to do your most difficult moves at first. Gradually, as the boots begin to bend you will be able to do more.

When lacing new skates, leave the top hook unlaced. This will allow you to bend your ankle more easily. Later, when the boots soften up, you should lace the top hooks.

Put on blade guards and wear the skates around the house. Alternate 15 minutes on, 15 minutes off.

Put on a pair of wet socks and then put the skates on. Wear the skates for a while.

10. HOW OFTEN SHOULD BLADES BE SHARPENED?

Frequency depends on how often you skate. It's time to have blades sharpened if they slip sideways or if an edge slips when you try to push.

When you run your finger lightly along the bottom of the blade, you should feel a hollow and two smooth edges. If the edges are rounded or rough, have the blades sharpened.

Blades get dull faster and sometimes are damaged if you walk around an arena without blade guards. To protect your blades, never walk on hard or dirty surfaces such as concrete, metal or tile without guards.

Be aware that all sharpenings are not equal. There is a broad range in the quality of the work done by people who sharpen skates. At some rinks, the sharpeners only know how to do hockey skates and rental skates. Make sure the sharpener knows how to sharpen figure skates. Expensive figure skating blades must have a custom sharpening. It's worth a few dollars extra.

Do not allow a sharpener to shave off the bottom toe pick — even if you have tripped over it. You won't be able to jump and spin without toe picks.

11. I WANT MY SKATES TO LAST A LONG TIME. HOW SHOULD I TAKE CARE OF MY SKATES?

Have the soles of new skates waterproofed with wax or heel-and-sole enamel. These products are available in pro shops.

Always wear blade guards when you are off the ice.

Always use a towel or chamois to wipe the moisture off the blades and soles of the boot after you skate. Some skaters put protective terry cloth covers over the blades when storing their skates.

Never store your skates with guards on the blades. The moisture in the guards may cause your blades to rust.

Keep your skates clean. They will stay looking new longer, and you will treat them as if they were new. Use polish made for skates.

Tighten the screws in the base of the blades occasionally. With normal wear and tear, the screws sometimes loosen.

Keep skates, chamois, guards, blade covers, boot covers and other accessories in one skate bag. Then you will not have to spend time rounding up equipment when it's time to go skating.

Remove your skates from the bag when you get home, and store them in a dry place. This will allow the soles to dry completely between skating sessions.

12. WHAT SHOULD I WEAR WHILE I PRACTICE?

Temperatures vary widely from rink to rink. You should dress for warmth and comfort.

Hats, gloves, sweaters and jackets may be necessary, depending on the temperature. Wear layers that can be removed as you warm up.

For extra padding and warmth, tots always should wear a hat and gloves. Depending on the rink temperature, they may need a snowsuit.

Your outfit should be loose enough or stretchy to allow unconstricted movement. Avoid pants and shirts that are too baggy or too tight.

Many girls and women prefer to wear a short skirt or dress designed for skating and tights.

Male figure skaters typically wear warm up pants, a comfortable well-fitted shirt and a sweater or light jacket.

Chapter 3
Basics

*I*n this chapter instructions are given for doing basic figure skating skills. These skills are the foundation of the sport, so take your time and learn them well. When you have mastered these skills, you will be ready to learn free skating (jumps and spins), figures and ice dancing.

It's important that you learn to do the skills in the order presented. That way, you'll make steady, safe progress toward your goals. Use the checklist and check off each skill as you learn it.

Each skill is explained step by step. The instructions for many of the skills are followed by Sharpen Your Skills, which is a tip to help you learn the skill or an exercise to use the skill.

In the instructions, references are made to the "skating" foot and the "free" foot. The skating foot is the foot that is on the ice. The free foot is the one not on the ice.

You also should be aware that the bottom of a skate blade is concave and therefore has two edges, inside and outside. The outside edge is toward the outside of the foot, and the inside edge is toward the inside of your foot.

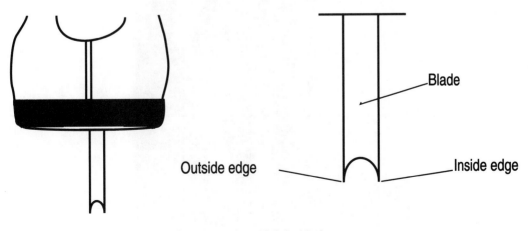

Cross-section of right blade

GETTING STARTED

If this is your first attempt at skating, it is a good idea to put on your skates and blade guards and practice marching, falling and getting up on a floor before you try it on the ice. This will help you get used to balancing on thin blades on a surface that's not slippery.

Unfortunately, falling is as much a part of skating as graceful gliding. No one learns to skate well without taking a few tumbles. It's important to learn to fall correctly to reduce the risk of hurting yourself.

STEPPING ONTO THE ICE

1. Standing outside the doorway to the ice, remove guards from blades.
2. Holding onto the boards, place one foot and then the other foot on the ice.
3. Still holding onto the boards with one hand, take a few tiny steps, picking up your feet, as if you were marching.
4. Carefully move away from the boards.

FALLING DOWN AND GETTING UP

1. Bend your knees until your hips are close to the ice. Hold your hands and arms at chest height, as if pressing on a table. Keep your head forward with your chin tucked toward your chest.
2. Fall to one buttock. Do not reach down to the ice with your hands to cushion the fall.
3. To get up as quickly as possible, roll over to your hands and knees.
4. Keeping your hands on the ice, place one foot between your hands, with the blade flat on the ice.
5. Slowly stand up, and place your other foot on the ice. Hold your hands in front of your body for balance.

step 2   step 4   step 5

FIRST STEPS

1. Stand tall with your head up and hold your arms out to your sides and slightly in front, as if pressing on a table. Your ankles should be straight, not leaning in or out. Place your feet about hip-width apart.
2. March in place. Make sure you don't disturb your upper body when you lift your legs.
3. March forward, taking small steps.

Sharpen Your Skills:
Gradually try to glide a little longer on each foot.

GLIDE ON TWO FEET
1. March forward to gain speed.
2. Put your feet in parallel position about hip-width apart and glide. Slightly bend your knees. Your weight should be evenly balanced on both feet, slightly behind the middle of the blades. Extend your arms to your sides and slightly forward, as if pressing your hands on a table.

Important: This is the "feet-together position," which will be referred to in the instructions for other skills.

Sharpen Your Skills:
To glide in a straight line, you need to keep your head up, shoulders level and hips level.

DIP

1. Glide on two feet with your arms extended in front of your body.
2. Bend your knees to lower your hips until they are slightly higher than your knees.
3. Keep your back straight but angled slightly forward at the hips to maintain balance. You should feel as if you are sitting in a chair.

Sharpen Your Skills:

Look where you are going, not down at the ice.

See how low you can dip your hips and still maintain your balance.

FISHIES

Fishies are also known as sculling and swizzles.

1. Glide on two feet.
2. Let your toes glide forward and outward until slightly more than hip-width apart. Bend your knees as you make this V-shape with your feet.
3. Angle both toes inward while straightening your knees and pulling feet together in a parallel position to continue gliding.
4. Repeat Steps 2 and 3 to move across the ice.

step 2　　　　　step 3

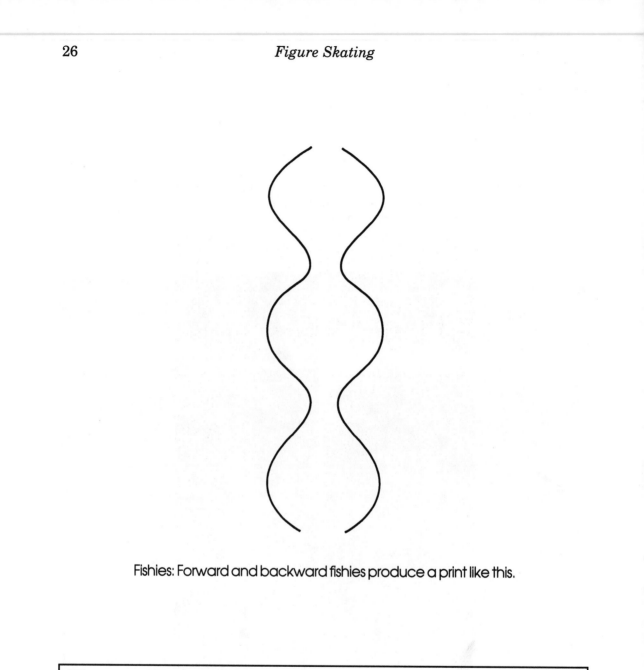

Fishies: Forward and backward fishies produce a print like this.

Sharpen Your Skills:

Try to gain speed as you do fishies across the rink. Vigorous knee action will help.

Don't let your head and shoulders dip forward every time your feet glide apart.

Just for fun: Do fishies of various sizes. Make little fishies by keeping your feet close together. Make large fishies — call them whales or sharks — letting your feet go as far apart as possible before drawing your toes together.

SNOWPLOW STOP

A snowplow stop in skating is similar to a snowplow stop in skiing. You will skid to a stop with your feet in a wide V-shape.

1. Glide on two feet.
2. Bend your knees and turn your toes inward, applying pressure to the inside edges of the blades. Press your heels outward as your blades slide or skid to a stop.

Sharpen Your Skills:

When you can do a snowplow stop slowly, try moving a little faster into the stop. Keep your head up, bend your knees and don't lean forward over your toes.

Do not try to touch your knees or your toes together as you stop.

ONE-FOOT SNOWPLOW STOP

1. Glide forward on two feet.
2. Bend both knees and let one foot slide slightly forward and to the side until you skid to a stop. Your weight should shift toward the foot that is skidding. The other foot continues to point straight ahead.

Right one-foot snowplow stop

Sharpen Your Skills:

When you can do a one-foot snowplow stop with your right foot, try it with your left foot.

Keep your shoulders and hips square to the direction you are moving; don't turn to the side as you stop.

BACKWARD WIGGLES

1. Stand with your feet hip-width apart and slightly pigeon-toed. Bend your knees slightly, balancing with your weight over the balls of the feet. Extend your arms to your sides and slightly forward.
2. Moving your hips from side to side, as if you are doing the 1960s dance the Twist, move backward across the ice.

   In other words: Transfer your weight from the inside edge of one blade to the inside edge of the other to move backward in a zigzag motion. Do not lift your feet off the ice.

step 2   step 2

Sharpen Your Skills:

If you try to wiggle but you don't move, try this to get some momentum: Face the wall and gently push yourself away from the wall before starting the wiggling motion.

To encourage children to move backward, tell them to pretend they are puppies wagging their tails.

BACKWARD GLIDE ON TWO FEET
1. Gain speed by doing back wiggles.
2. Put your feet in parallel position about hip-width apart and glide. Extend your arms to your sides and hold your head up.

Sharpen Your Skills:
Make sure you glide on the balls of your feet, slightly in front of the middle of the blades. If you lean too far forward, your toe picks will scratch the ice and slow you down.

BACKWARD FISHIES
1. Stand with your feet slightly pigeon-toed with your weight over the balls of the feet.
2. As you bend your knees, let your heels glide apart in a V-shape a little more than hip-width apart.
3. Straighten your knees while drawing both heels together, letting your feet glide into parallel position.
4. Repeat Steps 2 and 3 to move across the ice.

step 2   step 3

Sharpen Your Skills:
Try to gain speed as you do fishies across the ice. Vigorous knee action will help.

FORWARD GLIDE ON ONE FOOT
1. Glide forward on two feet.
2. Lift one foot and shift your weight slightly over the gliding foot. Hold the free foot against the ankle of your skating leg.

Sharpen Your Skills:
Practice gliding on your left foot as well as on your right foot.

Glide in a straight line. You will curve if your shoulders or hips are uneven. Also, your hips and shoulders should face forward.

Try this exercise if you are uneasy about lifting one foot: Stand with one hand resting on the boards. As you lift one foot, take your hand off the boards. Balance for a second or two before touching the boards again.

STROKING

Skating forward is also called "stroking." You should practice stroking every time you skate.

1. Stand in the feet-together position: Extend your arms to your sides and slightly forward as if pressing on a table. Hold your head up and place your feet hip-width apart.
2. To push, press one blade to the inside edge and push against the ice in an outward motion until the leg is fully extended and your free toe is pointed and angled toward the ice. As you push, the other leg will glide forward. Your weight is just behind the middle of the blade.
3. Rise on your knees as you return to the feet-together position.
4. Re-bend your knees and push with the other foot; extend until leg is straight. Keep your hips facing forward; do not open your hip with each push.
5. Move across the ice pushing with one foot and then the other.

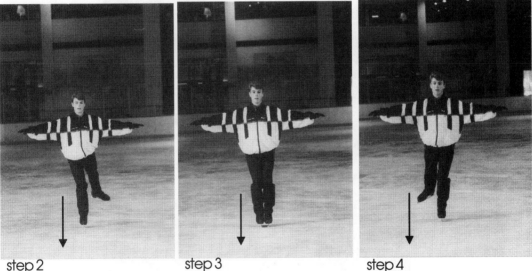

step 2   step 3   step 4

Sharpen Your Skills:

When stroking across the rink, concentrate on bending the skating knee to get a strong push.

Be careful not to push with your toe picks, use the inside edge of the blade.

Concentrate on your posture: Keep your upper body still. Keep your shoulders over your hips. Don't lunge forward with every step.

BACKWARD GLIDE ON ONE FOOT
1. Glide backward on two feet.
2. Lift one foot and shift your weight over the gliding foot. Hold your free foot against the ankle of the skating leg.

Sharpen Your Skills:
Practice until you can glide equally well on either foot.

Hold your shoulders level and your hips level as you glide.

FORWARD SCULLING
Sculling, also called pumping, will prepare you to do crossovers. Review forward fishies, page 25.

1. Glide forward on two feet counterclockwise on a circle.
2. Turn your upper body and arms toward the center of the circle. Hold your right arm in front at hip height, with palm down, over the circle. Hold your left arm behind at hip height, with palm down, over the circle. Look in the direction you are going.
3. Emphasizing an up-and-down motion with your knees, perform a sculling motion (fishies) with your right foot. Most of your weight should be over the left foot, which is gliding.
4. Also, practice sculling clockwise on a circle, with your left arm leading and your left foot sculling.

step 2

step 3

step 3

Sharpen Your Skills:
Make sure you don't lift off the ice the foot that is doing the sculling. Use your entire inside edge, not the toe picks, to push.

FORWARD CROSSOVERS
Doing crossovers is a powerful, efficient way to skate on a curve.

1. Glide forward on two feet counterclockwise on a circle.
2. Turn your upper body and arms toward the center of the circle. Hold your right arm in front at hip height, with palm down, over the circle. Hold your left arm behind at hip height, with palm down, over the circle.
3. Stroke with your right leg. Cross your right foot over your left foot, and place it on the ice on the inside edge, keeping your feet parallel. Your right knee will be bent when you place your right foot on the ice.
4. Push your left leg under the right and lift the left blade parallel to the ice.
5. Then return your left foot to the feet-together position.
6. Repeat Steps 3-5 (alternating pushes with your right and left feet) as you move around the circle.
7. When you can do crossovers counterclockwise, practice them clockwise, with your left foot crossing over the right. Turn your upper body toward the center of the circle and extend your left arm forward.

step 3

step 4

step 5

Sharpen Your Skills:
If you are hesitant about crossing your feet, try this exercise: Face the boards and put your right hand on it. Take a small step to the left with your left foot. Cross your right foot over the left. Repeat the two steps, moving to the left. Be sure to keep your feet parallel and pointing at the wall. Also, try this exercise moving to the right, with your left foot crossing over the right.

When doing forward crossovers, avoid these common errors:
• Swinging the crossing foot wide before crossing over.
• Pushing with your toe picks. Each push should use the entire blade except the toe picks.
• Stepping ahead of the feet-together position with the inside foot.
• Holding your legs straight and stiff. The more the skating knee bends, the better.
• Gliding for a long time on two feet between crossovers.

BACKWARD SCULLING
Backward sculling is an exercise that will prepare you for backward crossovers.

1. Glide backward on two feet counterclockwise on a circle.
2. Turn your upper body and arms toward the center of the circle. Hold your left arm in front of your body at hip height, with palm down, over the circle. Hold your right arm in back of your body at hip height, palm down, over the circle. Look back over your right shoulder.
3. Emphasizing an up-and-down motion with the knees, perform a sculling motion (fishies) with your left foot. Your left foot is slightly pigeon-toed as it pushes; do not lift it off the ice. Most of your weight is over your right foot, which is gliding backward.
4. Also, practice backward sculling moving clockwise, with your left arm behind your body and your right foot sculling. Look back over your left shoulder.

step 2   step 3   step 3

Sharpen Your Skills:
Make sure you aren't leaning out of the circle, over the sculling foot.

The sculling foot should push forward, at an outward angle, opposite the direction of travel.

Bring your feet close together after each sculling motion. But do not pull the sculling foot around the heel of the gliding foot.

To prevent accidents, look in the direction you are moving.

BACK CROSSOVERS

1. Glide backward on two feet counterclockwise on a circle.
2. Turn your upper body toward the center of the circle. Hold your left arm in front of your body at hip height, with palm down, over the circle. Hold your right arm behind your body at hip height, with palm down, over the circle. Look back over your right shoulder.
3. Stroke with your left leg, pushing with a one-foot sculling motion.
4. Keeping your left foot on the ice, slide it heel first across and in front of your right foot.
5. Push your right leg under your left leg and out of the circle.
6. Then lift your right foot and return it to the uncrossed feet-together position.
7. Repeat steps 3-6 as you travel around the circle.
8. When you can do back crossovers counterclockwise, practice them clockwise with your right foot crossing in front of your left foot. Turn your upper body toward the center of the circle and extend your left arm behind your body. Look back over your left shoulder.

step 3   step 5   step 6

Sharpen Your Skills:

Bend your knees deeply as you do back crossovers.

If you hear scratching, sit back enough to take the pressure off your toe picks. Your weight should be slightly in front of the middle of the blades.

HOCKEY STOP

This stop is used by both hockey players and figure skaters.

1. Glide forward on two feet with your knees slightly bent. Hold your shoulders square to the line of travel. Extend your arms to your sides.
2. Without moving your upper body, turn your hips and skates sharply to the left. Bend your knees more deeply and skid to a stop. As you skid, keep your weight over both blades.
3. Try stopping by turning your hips and skates to the right.

step 3

Sharpen Your Skills:

Keep your upper body still and facing in the direction of travel as you attempt to stop, or you will glide in a circle instead of stopping.

Do the hockey stop slowly at first. Gradually add speed as you gain confidence. A fast hockey stop will produce an impressive spray of snow.

As you skid to a stop, the forward blade will skid on the inside edge, the back blade will skid on the outside edge.

T-STOP

A T-stop gets its name from the position of your feet: they form a letter T. A T-stop is more attractive than a snowplow stop.

1. Glide forward on two feet. Hold your right arm slightly in front and your left arm to your side. Hold your shoulders square to the line of travel.
2. Lift your right foot and glide on your left foot.
3. Open your right toe to the right and place your right foot on the ice behind the left, forming a letter T. Place the right blade on the outside edge and gently press your weight on it until you skid to a stop.
4. Also, practice stopping with your left foot making the top of the T. Hold your left arm slightly in front.

Sharpen Your Skills:

Keep your hips level, or you might curve as you stop.

Press your entire blade evenly on the ice as you stop; don't drag your toe picks.

TURN ON TWO FEET, FORWARD TO BACKWARD

1. Glide forward on two feet counterclockwise on a circle.
2. Turn your upper body and arms toward the center of the circle. Hold your right arm in front at hip height, with palm down, over the circle. Hold your left arm behind at hip height, with palm down, over the circle. Look in the direction you are moving.
3. Turn your toes into the circle and quickly twist your hips 180 degrees.
4. Keep your shoulders and arms facing into the circle and continue gliding backward. This is called a "checked" position, because you are checking, or stopping, the rotation. Continue to look in the direction you are moving.
5. When you can turn comfortably to the left, try turning to the right. Glide clockwise on a circle. Turn your upper body to the right and twist your hips to the right.

step 4   step 2

Sharpen Your Skills:

Bend your knees before the turn, rise to turn and re-bend after the turn.

While gliding into the turn, your weight is behind the middle of the blades. As you turn, your weight shifts over the balls of your feet.

You should not lose speed when you turn. If you do slow down, rotate your shoulders more in the direction you want to turn. Also, try to twist your hips quickly.

EDGES

You know how to glide on one foot going in a straight line. Now you need to learn to skate on one edge of your blade so you can glide on a curve. Remember, your blade is concave on the bottom, so it has two edges, an inside edge and an outside edge.

RIGHT FORWARD OUTSIDE (RFO) EDGE

1. Glide on two feet clockwise on a circle.
2. Turn your upper body and arms toward the center of the circle. Hold your left arm in front at hip height, with palm down, over the circle. Hold your right arm behind at hip height, palm down, over the circle. Look in the direction of travel.
3. Lift your left foot and hold it at your right heel. Transfer your weight to your right foot and glide on the outside edge, maintaining the curve. The skating knee is slightly bent.

step 3

LEFT FORWARD OUTSIDE (LFO) EDGE

1. Glide on two feet counterclockwise on a circle.
2. Turn your upper body and arms toward the center of the circle. Hold your right arm in front at hip height, with palm down, over the circle. Hold your left arm behind at hip height, with palm down, over the circle. Look in the direction of travel.
3. Lift your right foot and hold it at your left heel. Transfer your weight to your left foot and glide on the outside edge, maintaining the curve. The skating knee is slightly bent.

step 3

Sharpen Your Skills — Right and Left Forward Outside Edges:

Hold your body tall; do not bend at the waist or hips.

Hold the free foot parallel to the skating foot. Don't let the free toe and knee point out of the circle.

RIGHT FORWARD INSIDE (RFI) EDGE

1. Glide on two feet counterclockwise on a circle.
2. Turn your upper body and arms toward the center of the circle. Hold your right arm in front at hip height, with palm down, over the circle. Hold your left arm behind at hip height, with palm down, over the circle. Look in the direction of travel.
3. Lift your left foot and hold it at your right heel. Transfer your weight to your right foot and glide on the inside edge, maintaining the curve. The skating knee is slightly bent.

step 3

LEFT FORWARD INSIDE (LFI) EDGE

1. Glide on two feet counterclockwise on a circle.
2. Turn your upper body and arms toward the center of the circle. Hold your left arm in front at hip height, with palm down, over the circle. Hold your right arm behind at hip height, with palm down, over the circle. Look in the direction of travel.
3. Lift your right foot and hold it at your left heel. Transfer your weight to your left foot and glide on the inside edge, maintaining the curve. The skating knee is slightly bent.

step 3

Sharpen Your Skills — Right and Left Forward Inside Edges:
Hold the free foot parallel to the skating foot. Don't let the free toe and knee open into the circle.

RIGHT BACK OUTSIDE (RBO) EDGE

1. Glide backward on two feet counterclockwise on a circle.
2. Turn your upper body toward the center of the circle. Look into the circle. Hold your right arm behind your body, at hip height, with palm down, over the circle. Hold your left arm in front of your body at hip height, with palm down, over the circle.
3. Lift your left foot and hold your left toe at your right heel. Transfer your weight to your right foot and glideon the outside edge, maintaining the curve. The skating knee is slightly bent.

step 3

LEFT BACK OUTSIDE (LBO) EDGE

1. Glide backward on two feet clockwise on a circle.
2. Turn your upper body toward the center of the circle. Look into the circle. Hold your left arm behind your body at hip height, with palm down, over the circle. Hold your right arm in front of your body at hip height, with palm down, over the circle.
3. Lift your right foot and hold your right toe at your left heel. Transfer your weight to your left foot and glide on the outside edge, maintaining the curve. The skating knee is slightly bent.

step 3

Sharpen Your Skills — Right and Left Back Outside Edges:
If you hear a scratching noise, you are leaning too far forward on your blade.

RIGHT BACK INSIDE (RBI) EDGE

1. Glide backward on two feet clockwise on a circle.
2. Turn your upper body toward the center of the circle. Look into the circle. Hold your left arm behind your body at hip height, with palm down, over the circle. Hold your right arm in front of your body at hip height, with palm down, over the circle.
3. Lift your left foot and hold your left toe at your right heel. Transfer your weight to your right foot and glide on the inside edge, maintaining the curve. The skating knee is slightly bent.

step 3

LEFT BACK INSIDE (LBI) EDGE

1. Glide backward on two feet counterclockwise on a circle.
2. Turn your upper body toward the center of the circle. Look into the circle. Hold your right arm behind your body at hip height, with palm down, over the circle. Hold your left arm in front of your body at hip height, with palm down, over the circle.
3. Lift your right foot and hold your right toe at your left heel. Transfer your weight to your left foot and glide on the inside edge, maintaining the curve. The skating knee is slightly bent.

step 3

Sharpen Your Skills — Right and Left Back Inside Edges:

If you hear scratching noises, you are leaning too far forward on your blade.

Hold your free leg parallel to the skating leg as you glide on the edge. It will be difficult to control the edge if you pigeon-toe the free foot or allow it to point toward the center of the circle.

THREE TURNS

This turn is called a three because the print on the ice looks like a numeral 3.

Three turns are turns from forward to backward or backward to forward on one foot. As you turn you change from an inside edge to an outside edge, or an outside to an inside.

Forward threes are turned with the body weight on the ball of the blade. Back threes are turned with the body weight on the back of the blade.

This is the print of a Right Forward Outside Three Turn. At the turn, the skater changes edges, but not feet.

RIGHT FORWARD OUTSIDE (RFO) THREE TURN

1. Glide forward on two feet clockwise on a circle.
2. Turn your upper body and arms toward the center of the circle. Hold your left arm in front at hip height, with palm down, over the circle. Hold your right arm behind at hip height, with palm down, over the circle. Look in the direction of travel.
3. Lift your left foot and hold it at your right heel. Glide on the left forward outside edge.
4. Without moving your shoulders, turn your hips and right toe into the circle, allowing your hips to twist 180 degrees. Your blade will change from the RFO edge to the RBI edge.
5. Glide on the RBI edge. Keep your upper body facing into the circle and your arms extended over the circle in a checked position. Continue to look in the direction of travel.

step 3

step 5

LEFT FORWARD OUTSIDE (LFO) THREE TURN

1. Glide forward on two feet counterclockwise on a circle.
2. Turn your upper body and arms toward the center of the circle. Hold your right arm in front at hip height, with palm down, over the circle. Hold your left arm behind at hip height, with palm down, over the circle. Look in the direction of travel.
3. Lift your right foot and hold it at your left heel. Glide on the left forward outside edge.
4. Without moving your shoulders, turn your hips and left toe into the circle, allowing your hips to twist 180 degrees. As you turn, your blade changes from the LFO edge to the LBI edge.
5. Glide on the LBI edge. Keep your upper body facing into the circle and your arms extended over the circle in a checked position. Continue to look in the direction of travel.

step 5   step 3

Sharpen Your Skills — Right and Left Forward Outside Three Turns:

Avoid leaning forward over your toe pick as you turn. Keep your body upright; do not bend at the hips or waist.

Bend the skating knee slightly before the turn, rise on the knee to turn and re-bend the skating knee after the turn. Your weight will shift forward to the ball of your foot as you turn.

Do not move your free foot before, during or after the turn. Your free foot will remain at the heel of your skating foot.

After the turn, try to glide as far as possible on the back inside edge. It will be necessary to maintain a strongly checked position.

RIGHT FORWARD INSIDE (RFI) THREE TURN

1. Glide forward on two feet counterclockwise on a circle.
2. Turn your upper body and arms toward the center of the circle. Hold your right arm in front at hip height, with palm down, over the circle. Hold your left arm behind at hip height, with palm down, over the circle. Look in the direction of travel.
3. Lift your left foot and hold it at the inside of your right heel. Glide on the right forward inside edge.
4. Without moving your shoulders, turn your hips and left toe into the circle, allowing your hips to twist 180 degrees. As you turn, your blade changes from the RFI edge to the RBO edge.
5. Glide on the RBO edge. Keep your upper body facing into the circle and your arms extended over the circle in a checked position. Continue to look in the direction of travel.

step 3

step 5

LEFT FORWARD INSIDE (LFI) THREE TURN

1. Glide forward on two feet clockwise on a circle.
2. Turn your upper body and arms toward the center of the circle. Hold your left arm in front at hip height, with palm down, over the circle. Hold your right arm behind at hip height, with palm down, over the circle. Look in the direction of travel.
3. Lift your right foot and hold it at the inside of your left heel. Glide on the left forward inside edge.
4. Without moving your shoulders, turn your hips and left toe into the circle, allowing your hips to twist 180 degrees. As you turn, your blade changes from the LFI edge to the LBO edge.
5. Glide on the LBO edge. Keep your upper body facing into the circle and your arms extended over the circle in a checked position. Continue to look in the direction you are moving.

step 3

step 5

Sharpen Your Skills — Right and Left Forward Inside Three Turns:

Bend your skating knee slightly before the turn, rise on the knee to turn and re-bend after.

Glide as far as possible on the back outside edge after the turn. It will be necessary to maintain a strongly checked position.

MOHAWK

A mohawk is a turn from forward to backward or backward to forward, stepping from one foot to the other. Both steps are on the same edge, inside to inside or outside to outside. Here are the instructions for the most commonly used mohawks, the forward inside mohawks.

This is the print of a Right Forward Inside Mohawk. When turning, the skater changes feet.

RIGHT FORWARD INSIDE (RFI) MOHAWK

1. Glide on a right forward inside edge.
2. Turn your upper body and arms toward the center of the circle. Hold your right arm in front at hip height, with palm down, over the circle. Hold your left arm behind at hip height, with palm down, over the circle. Look in the direction of travel.
3. Open the toe of your left foot and hold your left heel at the instep of your right foot.
4. Turn your hips and right toe into the circle as you place your left foot on the ice, gliding on the left back inside edge.
5. Extend your right leg behind with your right toe slightly open and pointed. As you glide on the LBI edge, keep your shoulders and hips facing into the circle and your arms extended over the circle in a checked position. Continue to look in the direction of travel.

step 5   step 3   step 2

LEFT FORWARD INSIDE (LFI) MOHAWK

1. Glide on a left forward inside edge.
2. Turn your upper body and arms toward the center of the circle. Hold your left arm in front at hip height, with palm down, over the circle. Hold your right arm behind at hip height, with palm down, over the circle. Look in the direction of travel.
3. Open the toe of your right foot and hold your right heel at the instep of your left foot.
4. Turn your hips and left toe into the circle as you place your right foot on the ice, gliding on the right back inside edge.
5. Extend your left leg behind with your left toe slightly open and pointed. As you glide on the RBI edge, keep your shoulders and hips facing into the circle and your arms extended over the circle in a checked position. Continue to look in the direction of travel.

step 2 step 3 step 5

Sharpen Your Skills — Right and Left Forward Inside Mohawks:

Twist your hips quickly at the point of the turn.

Rise on your knee on the forward inside edge to turn and bend your knee as you step onto the back inside edge.

Practice doing a mohawk while holding onto the boards: Stand facing the boards with your arms extended to your sides and your hands on the boards. Stand on one foot and practice turning your hips and placing the free foot on the ice, turning from forward to backward.

When you feel confident with the mohawk turn, increase your speed going into the turn. Try doing forward crossovers before a mohawk.

RIGHT BACK OUTSIDE (RBO) THREE TURN

1. Glide backward on two feet counterclockwise on a circle.
2. Turn your upper body and arms counterclockwise to face out of the circle. Hold your left arm behind your body at hip height, with palm down, over the circle. Hold your right arm in front of your body, with palm down, outside the circle. Look back over your left shoulder.
3. Lift your left foot in front and in line with your right foot, which is gliding on the right back outside edge.
4. Without moving your shoulders, turn your hips and right heel into the circle, rock toward your heel and allow your hips to twist 180 degrees. As you turn, your blade changes from the RBO edge to the RFI edge.
5. Glide on the RFI edge. Hold your left foot pointed in front and slightly to the inside of your right foot. Keep your upper body facing out of the circle and your arms extended over the circle in a checked position. Continue to look in the direction of travel.

step 5   step 3

LEFT BACK OUTSIDE (LBO) THREE TURN

1. Glide backward on two feet clockwise on a circle.
2. Turn your upper body and arms clockwise to face out of the circle. Hold your right arm behind your body at hip height, with palm down, over the circle. Hold your left arm in front of your body, with palm down, outside the circle. Look back over your right shoulder.
3. Lift your right foot in front and in line with your left foot, which is gliding on the left back outside edge.
4. Without moving your shoulders, turn your hips and left heel into the circle, rock toward your heel and allow your hips to twist 180 degrees. As you turn, your blade changes from the LBO edge to the LFI edge.
5. Glide on the LFI edge. Hold your right foot pointed in front and slightly to the inside of your right foot. Keep your upper body facing out of the circle and your arms extended over the circle in a checked position. Continue to look in the direction of travel.

step 3

step 5

Sharpen Your Skills — Right and Left Back Outside Three Turns:

Keep your thighs close together before, during and after the turn. Don't let your free foot swing wide as you turn.

Bend your skating knee before the turn, rise on the knee to turn and re-bend after. Rock toward your heel as you turn.

Try to do a series of three turns on one foot: Do a forward inside three turn and then a back outside three turn.

RIGHT BACK INSIDE (RBI) THREE TURN

1. Glide backward on two feet clockwise on a circle.
2. Turn your upper body and arms clockwise to face out of the circle. Hold your right arm behind your body at hip height, with palm down, over the circle. Hold your left arm in front of your body and outside the circle, at hip height with palm down. Look back over your right shoulder.
3. Lift your left foot in front, slightly pigeon-toed and in line with your right foot, which is gliding on the right back inside edge.
4. Without moving your shoulders, turn your hips and right heel into the circle, rock toward your heel and allow your hips to twist 180 degrees. As you turn, your blade changes from the RBI edge to the RFO edge.
5. Glide on the RFO edge. Hold your left foot pointed in front. Keep your upper body facing out of the circle and your arms extended over the circle in a checked position. Continue to look in the direction of travel.

step 3

step 5

LEFT BACK INSIDE (LBI) THREE TURN

1. Glide backward on two feet counterclockwise on a circle.
2. Turn your upper body and arms counterclockwise to face out of the circle. Hold your left arm behind your body at hip height, with palm down over the circle. Hold your right arm in front of your body and outside the circle, at hip height with palm down. Look back over your left shoulder.
3. Lift your right foot in front, slightly pigeon-toed and in line with your left foot, which is gliding on the left back inside edge.
4. Without moving your shoulders, turn your hips and left heel into the circle, rock toward your heel and allow your hips to twist 180 degrees. As you turn, your blade changes from the LBI edge to the LFO edge.
5. Glide on the LFO edge. Hold your right foot pointed in front. Keep your upper body facing out of the circle and your arms extended over the circle in a checked position. Continue to look in the direction of travel.

step 5

step 3

> ## *Sharpen Your Skills — Right and Left Back Inside Three Turns:*
> Keep your thighs close together before, during and after the turn.
>
> Bend your skating knee before the turn, rise on the knee to turn and re-bend after. Rock toward your heel as you turn.

CHAPTER 3 BASICS CHECKLIST

These skills are the fundamentals of figure skating. Learn them in the order listed, from easiest to most difficult. As you master a skill, check it off and move on to the next skill.

__Stepping onto the ice
__Falling down and getting up
__First steps
__Glide on two feet
__Dip
__Fishies
__Snowplow stop
__One-foot snowplow stop, right and left

__Backward wiggles
__Backward glide on two feet
__Backward fishies
__Forward glide on one foot, right and left
__Forward stroking
__Backward glide on one foot, right and left

__Forward sculling, right and left   -
__Forward crossovers, right and left
__Backward sculling, right and left
__Backward crossovers, right and left
__Hockey stop
__T-stop, right and left
__Turn on two feet , forward to backward

Edges:
    __RFO edge
    __LFO edge
    __RFI edge
    __LFI edge
    __RBO edge
    __LBO edge
    __RBI edge
    __LBI edge
Three turns (forward)
    __RFO three turn
    __LFO three turn
    __RFI three turn
    __LFI three turn
Mohawks
    __RFI mohawk
    __LFI mohawk

Three turns (backward)
    __RBO three turn
    __LBO three turn
    __RBI three turn
    __LBI three turn

Chapter 4
Free Skating

INTRODUCTION TO FREE SKATING
Now that you've mastered basic steps and turns, you're ready to use your skills in free skating. Also known as freestyle, free skating includes a wide variety of jumps, spins, footwork and other moves.

Free skating is "free" in the sense that you may select the elements to include in a routine or program. The elements may be well-known moves or moves that you create. In some competitions and tests, certain jumps, spins and footwork are required, but you are free to arrange the elements in any way that you like.

This chapter , which has sections on jumps and spins, includes step-by-step instructions for doing basic free skating moves.

The Free Skating Checklist on page 115 lists the skills in the order I/WSA coaches usually teach them, from easiest to more difficult. The list includes a mixture of jumps and spins, because a free skater needs to have a balanced repertoire of jumps and spins at every level from beginning through advanced.

Members of the United States Figure Skating Association are eligible to take a series of eight free skating proficiency tests, ranging from Pre-Preliminary (1) through Senior (8). On each test, the skater must perform Moves in the Field, which involve stroking, edges and turns. Also, on each test, a skater must perform designated jumps, spins and step sequences. On Tests 2-8, the elements are performed in a program to music selected by the skater. Judges watch each test and decide if the skater passes or must retry the test at a later date.

The Ice Skating Institute of America offers a series of 10 freestyle tests. Specific jumps, spins and footwork, as well as a solo program to music, are required on each test. An instructor or judge determines whether a skater performs the elements well enough to pass.

FREE SKATING: BASIC MANEUVERS
There's more to free skating than jumps and spins. You also need to know some moves which can be used between jumps and spins in routines. Here are basic free-skating maneuvers that are fun to do: spiral, lunge, shoot the duck and pivot.

SPIRAL

Despite it's name, a spiral doesn't look anything like a spin. It is the skating version of ballet's arabesque. A spiral is a beautiful and versatile move. Your arms and head can be held in many different positions. A spiral can be done forward or backward on a straight line or on an edge. A spiral moving forward on a straight line is the easiest to accomplish.

1. Stroke forward and glide on two feet. Extend your arms to your sides at shoulder height.
2. Lift one leg behind to at least hip height. Holding the leg straight, open your knee and point your toe outward so the blade is parallel to the ice.
3. Keep your chin up and shoulders pressed back. Your body should make an upward curve from the top of the head to the foot.
4. Continue to glide on a straight leg with your weight on the back of the blade.

Sharpen Your Skills:

Before attempting a spiral, practice the position while resting both hands on the rink's boards. Lift one leg as high as possible behind you. Do not look down. Stay off the toe pick of the skating foot.

At first you may not feel comfortable lifting your free leg very high. Challenge yourself to lift it a little higher each time. Stretching exercises will help you do this.

Experiment with spirals on various edges, forward and backward. Caution: Before lifting your leg on a backward spiral, be sure no other skaters are in your way.

Experiment with arm positions. Be creative.

LUNGE

In a lunge, your free leg is extended behind, dragging on the ice.

1. Stroke forward and glide on two feet. Extend your arms to your sides at shoulder height.
2. Bend one knee while extending the other leg behind, dragging that boot on the ice. Hold your back up and lift your chin. Keep your shoulders facing forward and your hips level.

Sharpen Your Skills:

Try a lunge with the other leg dragging behind.

If you curve while lunging, you are probably dropping one hip. Make certain your hips are level.

SHOOT THE DUCK

This is a fun move with a fun name. The shoot the duck is seldom included in free skating routines, but it is a good balance exercise. It may give you confidence to try a sit spin later.

1. Glide forward on two feet. Extend both arms forward.
2. Bend both knees until your thighs are parallel to the ice.
3. Extend one foot forward so your leg is parallel to the ice. Point your toe so your heel doesn't catch in the ice.
4. Keep your weight pressed forward on the skating foot. Do not sit back on the heel of the skating foot.
5. To get up, bring the extended foot back, next to the skating foot, and stand up with your feet together.

step 2   step 3

Sharpen Your Skills:

Try to do a shoot the duck with the other foot extended forward.

Try to descend with one leg extended forward. Also, try to rise from a shoot the duck on one foot.

Try a shoot the duck moving backward or on an inside or outside edge.

FORWARD INSIDE PIVOT

A pivot is not technically a spin, but it is an attractive move that will help you learn to spin. There are several different pivots, in which the toe of one blade is planted at the center and the other foot rotates around the center. In the pivot explained here, the forward inside pivot, your left toe is the center and your right foot will glide counterclockwise on a forward inside edge.

1. Place your left toe pick in the ice. Bend your left knee and turn it out to the left. Extend your left arm in front and your right arm to your side.
2. Pump a few times with your right foot and move it around your left toe. Simultaneously, rotate your upper body to the left. Press your weight toward your left knee and toe, but don't lean over your toes.
3. Stop pumping and let your right foot glide in a large circle around your left toe. Continue to look to the left and lead with your left arm.

step 1

step 3

Sharpen Your Skills:

Do not pump constantly as you pivot; allow your right foot to glide around.

Make sure your left leg and foot are always turned out, with your left heel pointing toward the inside of your right foot. If you get out of position, the pivot will stall.

The more deeply you bend your left knee, the better your pivot will move and look.

You may glide only once around the circle at first. Practice until you can glide around two or more times.

INTRODUCTION TO SPINS

Spinning is one of the most fascinating parts of free skating to watch and to do. Some skaters reach amazing speeds and rotate dozens of times in a spin. While spinning, skaters can put their arms, legs and body in many different positions, some standard and some innovative.

Even though spinning looks like magic, you can learn to spin. It just takes time and practice to learn the positions. And, yes, you'll probably get dizzy. It happens whenever a spinner isn't balanced. Most skaters find that the dizziness goes away as their technique improves.

This section includes step-by-step instructions for doing basic spins, including two-foot, one-foot, back, sit and camel. As you learn each spin, check it off on the Free Skating Checklist, page 115.

Instructions are written for skaters who spin and jump counterclockwise (toward their left) since that is the most common way to spin. It's OK to spin clockwise if that is more natural for you.

If you're not sure which way is natural for you, here are a couple methods to help you decide:

1. Try turning one direction and then the other. One way will feel better.
2. Step up on a step. If you step up with your right leg, you should spin counterclockwise. If you step up with your left leg, spin clockwise.
3. Which foot would you use to kick a soccer ball? If you prefer to kick with your right foot, spin counterclockwise. If you prefer to kick with your left, spin clockwise.

If you decide to spin clockwise, switch the lefts and rights in the instructions for each spin.

STANDARD SPIN PREPARATION

Skaters use the same method to enter several different spins, including the one-foot, sit and camel spins. We will call this method the Standard Spin Preparation:

1. Do back crossovers clockwise on a small circle. (This is opposite the direction you do back crossovers to prepare for a waltz jump.)
2. On the final crossover, glide on the right back inside edge with your right knee deeply bent. Leave your left foot stretched under and behind your right foot, with your left toe pointing out of the circle.
3. Press your right arm back and hold your left arm across and in front of your body, so your torso twists and faces out of the circle.
4. Step into the circle on a tight left forward outside edge with your left knee deeply bent. As you step, look to the left and rotate your arms to the left.
5. Do a left forward outside three turn. The exit edge of the three turn is the left back inside edge on which you will spin, turning in small circles.

step 3

step 4

step 4

step 5
for upright
spin

The best spins are "centered" on one spot. When a spin is centered, the skater draws many circles, one on top of the other, with the blade. The circles are several inches in diameter. When the spin moves off the center, it "travels."

Traveling results whenever the spinner is not perfectly balanced over the correct part of the blade. It only takes a slight misalignment of shoulders, hips or arms to make a spin travel.

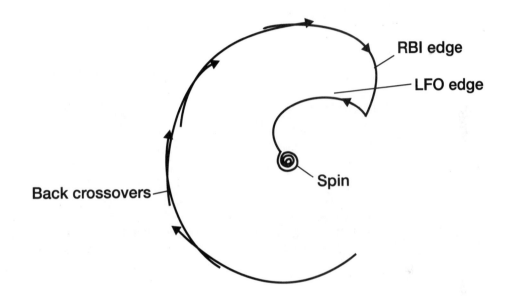

The Standard Spin Preparation consists of counterclockwise back crossovers, ending on a RBI edge, a step into the circle (created by the back crossovers) on a deep LFO edge. This spin is centered: The circles of the spin are round and on top of the initial three turn.

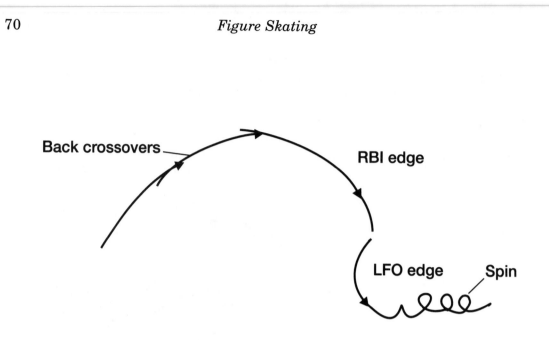

Traveling Spin — This is an example of an uncentered spin. The step to LFO edge was not into the circle. The spin travelled, drawing little loops instead of circles on the ice.

Here are some tips to help you center a spin:

1. When you step on the left forward outside edge to enter the spin, step into, not out of, the circle formed by the preparatory back crossovers.
2. Hold your shoulders level on the entry edge. Do not hunch your shoulders toward your ears as you spin.
3. Hold your body and head still once you reach the spinning position. If your weight shifts, your blade will draw loops instead of circles.
4. If you wobble and scratch too much with the bottom toe pick, your spin will slow down. The toe pick is used only for balance. Most of your weight should be on the ball of your foot.
5. Do NOT attempt to "twirl" on your toe pick. This is not the correct place to spin and it is dangerous to try to balance on the toe picks.

STANDARD SPIN EXIT

Skaters commonly use one method for moving out of a spin. We call this the Standard Spin Exit. The body position is very similar to the Standard Landing Position for jumps (Page 84).

1. As your spin slows down, push from the left back inside edge, on which you are spinning, to the right back outside edge. Bend your right knee as you glide out of the spin.
2. Extend your left leg behind with your toe pointed and open.
3. As you push out, extend your arms to your sides in a checked position. Hold your shoulders and hips square to the print of the right back outside edge.
4. Look forward (where you came from) with your chin up and over the center of your chest.

step 1

step 3

That Dizzy Feeling

Some skaters, especially beginners, get dizzy when they spin. Some people even feel a bit nauseous. The uncomfortable feeling is the result of pressure in the fluids in your inner ear, which controls balance.

As you practice spinning, your ears will become accustomed to the pressure and you won't get as dizzy. To prevent dizziness, work on your spinning technique: Keep your eyes open. Look straight ahead, but do not focus on one spot while spinning. Do not "spot" like a ballet dancer doing turns.

TWO-FOOT SPIN

Description:
 A spin in the upright position with both feet on the ice. Review forward inside pivot, page 66.

Preparation:
 1. Start with a forward inside pivot: Place your left toe pick in the ice. Extend your left arm in front and right arm to the side.
 2. Pump with your right foot to start it moving wide around your left toe.
 3. Rotate your upper body to the left.
 4. Stop pumping and pull your right foot closer to your left. Gently press your left foot down until the ball of the foot is on the ice.

step 1

Spin Position:
1. As you spin, make a circle with your arms at chest height, as if you are hugging a beach ball.
2. Grasp one hand with the other and pull both hands toward your chest, holding your elbows out.
3. Gently press your hands down the front of your body.
4. Stand tall as you spin with your weight balanced over both feet. Hold your chin up and look out over the center of your chest.

step 1

step 3

Exit:
1. Lift your right foot.
2. Push out, using the Standard Spin Exit: Push from the left back inside edge, on which you are spinning, to the right back outside edge. Bend your right knee as you glide out of the spin (see photos, page 71).
3. Extend your left leg back with your left toe pointed and open. Extend your arms to your sides in a checked position. Hold your shoulders and hips square to the print of the right back outside edge.
4. As you glide, look forward (where you came from) with your chin up and over the center of your chest.

Common errors:
1. Spinning too far back on your heels.
2. Spinning too far forward on your blades, with your toe picks scratching the ice.
3. Traveling. This can be caused by rotating your arms unevenly at the start of the spin, or allowing your shoulders to tilt.

Sharpen Your Skills:
Your goal is to spin as long and as fast as possible. If you can do two rotations now, try for three and then try for more. You can increase the number of rotations by rotating your arms smoothly and evenly into the spin and avoiding your toe picks while spinning.

TWO-FOOT TO ONE-FOOT SPIN

Description:
An upright spin starting on two feet and changing to one foot.

Preparation:
1. Start with a two-foot spin. Do several rotations to establish the spin.

Spin Position:
1. Carefully lift your right foot and balance your weight over the ball of your left foot. Your left leg should be straight, but not locked, while spinning.
2. Hold your right foot up with your toe touching the side of your left shin.
3. Hold your arms in a circle at chest height. Join hands and pull your hands toward the center of your chest.
4. Gently press your hands down the front of your body.

Exit:
1. Push out, using the Standard Spin Exit.

Common errors:
1. Holding your right (free) foot in an incorrect position: Do not hook your right toe behind your left calf. Do not keep your knees tight together and lift your right foot behind.
2. Allowing your arms, hands and head to shift to the right as you spin.

Sharpen Your Skills:
Try to increase the number of rotations you can do while spinning on one foot.

Spin position, step 3

ONE-FOOT SPIN

Description:
 A spin on one foot in the upright position.

Preparation:
 Use the Standard Spin Preparation:
 1. Do back crossovers clockwise on a small circle.
 2. On the final crossover, glide on the right back inside edge with your right knee deeply bent. Leave your left foot stretched under and behind your right foot, with your left toe pointing out of the circle.
 3. Pull your right arm back and behind and hold your left arm across and in front of your body, so your torso twists and faces out of the circle.
 4. Step into the circle on a tight left forward outside edge with your left knee deeply bent. As you step, look to the left and rotate your arms to the left.
 5. Do a left forward outside three turn.

Spin Position 1:
 1. Immediately after the three turn, straighten your left knee and begin to spin on the left back inside edge.
 2. Move your right leg wide around to the side until it is extended at an angle slightly in front of your body. Then bend your right knee and hold your right foot against your left shin.
 3. While bending your right knee, make a circle with your arms. Join hands and then pull your hands toward the center of your chest.

step 1

step 2

step 3

Spin Position 2:

This more-advanced position makes the one-foot spin a "scratch" spin. It gets its name from the way the bottom toe pick scratches the ice.

1. Step into the spin and straighten your left knee.
2. Swing your right leg wide around until it is rounded in front, with your foot about knee high. Hold your arms in an open circle.
3. Bend your right knee, crossing your right foot in front of your left leg. Hold your right heel to the left side of your left leg, just above your left knee.
4. As your right leg crosses in front, join hands and pull your hands toward the center of your chest.
5. Push your right heel down, touching your left leg, until both legs are straight. At the same time, push your hands down close to your body. As you push down with your hands and foot, you will gain speed.

step 2   step 4   step 5

Exit:

1. Lift your right foot and push out, using the Standard Spin Exit.

Common errors:

1. Stepping out of the circle created by the preparatory back crossovers when stepping on the left forward outside entry edge, making it difficult to center the spin.
2. Stepping into the spin with shoulders and arms not level.
3. Rocking on the blade, which causes traveling.
4. Spinning on the forward outside edge, instead of the back inside edge.

Sharpen Your Skills:

When you have mastered the first spin position, work on Spin Position 2. Spin Position 2 is more difficult but it will produce a faster, longer spin.

As you spin, you will feel pressure pushing out against your arms; this is centrifugal force. Pull your arms in, against the pressure, and you will spin faster.

BACK SPIN

Description:
   Skaters who do a one-foot spin on their left foot, do a back spin on their right foot. Forward and back spins both rotate in the same direction, counterclockwise. Review two-foot to one-foot spin.

Preparation:
   1. Start a two-foot spin, rotating several times to establish the spin.
   2. Form an open circle with your arms.

Spin Position 1:
   1. While spinning on two feet, pick up your left foot and hold it beside or in front of your right shin.
   2. Maintaining a strong upright position, with your weight over the ball of your right foot, spin on the right back outside edge.
   3. Join hands and pull both hands toward your chest.

Spin Position 2:
   When done in this more-advanced position, a back spin becomes a back scratch spin.
   1. Pick up your left leg and hold it rounded in front, with your left foot about knee high.
   2. Bend your left knee, crossing your left foot in front of your right leg at about knee height.
   3. As your left leg crosses in front, join hands and pull your hands toward your chest.
   4. Push your left heel down, touching your right leg, until both legs are straight. At the same time, push your hands down close to your body. As you push down, you will gain speed.

step 1

step 3

Exit:
1. Bend your right knee and push your left leg back.
2. Glide out of the spin on the right back outside edge, in the Standard Spin Exit position.

Common errors:
1. Bending forward from your hips during the spin.
2. Spinning on the right forward inside edge instead of the right back outside edge.
3. In Spin Position 2, holding the free leg too open as it crosses in front of the skating leg. Press the free hip forward.

Sharpen Your Skills:

1. Make sure you can do Spin Position 1 before you try Spin Position 2.

2. Try a change-foot spin: Start with a one-foot spin on your left foot. Without stopping, step down on your right foot and do a back spin.

3. Invest a lot of practice time in perfecting a back spin, because a back spin will help you understand and perform advanced jumps. Your position in a back spin is very similar to the position in which you rotate in double jumps.

4. Another way to exit a back spin is to move your left foot across your right and step down on the left back inside edge. Pull your right leg back and glide out of the spin on the LBI edge.

SIT SPIN
Description:
  A spin in a sitting position.

Preparation:
  1. Standard Spin Preparation.

Spin Position:
  1. As you step into the spin on the left forward outside edge, continue to bend your left knee.
  2. Swing your right foot around in a wide circle. As your right leg nears the front, turn it open slightly so the heel doesn't hit the ice. The swing of the right leg should be from high behind to low in front and as wide as possible.
  3. As your right leg swings around and your left knee bends to a sitting position, hold your arms open and arch your upper body forward. Bring your hands together just as the free leg finishes its swing.
  4. While spinning with your left knee deeply bent, hold your hands over or on the shin of the right leg, which is extended straight and low in front.
  5. Keep your head and shoulders up and back arched and pressed forward over the spinning (left) leg.

step 1

step 3

Exit:
1. Rise to a one-foot upright spin.
2. Push out using the Standard Spin Exit.

Common errors:
1. Stepping out of the circle created by the preparatory back crossovers when stepping on the left forward outside entry edge, making it difficult to center the spin.
2. Not swinging the free leg strongly and quickly from high to low.
3. Allowing the free foot to hook around the spinning foot. The free foot should not cross in front of the spinning foot.
4. Sitting too high or too low. If you sit too high, it doesn't count as a sit spin. If you squat too low, your back will be rounded unattractively.
5. Straightening your left knee before bending it for the sitting position.

Sharpen Your Skills:

Practice the shoot the duck (Page 65) to get used to the sit spin position. Try a left backward shoot the duck.

Most skaters do not sit very low on their first attempts at a sit spin. Challenge yourself to bend your left knee more deeply and sit lower. Try to bend until your left thigh is parallel to the ice.

CAMEL SPIN

Description:
 A spin in the spiral position. Review spiral, page 63.

Preparation:
 1. Standard Spin Preparation.

Spin Position:
 1. As you step onto the left forward outside entry edge and do the three turn, swing your left arm to the left, parallel to the ice. Look to the left and keep your chin up.
 2. Immediately after the left forward outside three turn, press up on your left knee and lift your right leg behind until it is parallel to the ice or higher.
 3. Turn out your right leg and point your right toe. Hold your head up and your arms extended like wings. Press your shoulders up and arch your back.

step 1

step 2

step 3

Exit:
   1. Raise your upper body and shift to an upright one-foot spin.
   2. Push out, using the Standard Spin Exit.

Common errors:
   1. Releasing your left arm and knee too quickly on the step into the spin.
   2. Entering the spin with your head and shoulders looking down at the ice.
   3. Spinning on the toe pick or heel, rather than the ball of the foot.
   4. Allowing your right toe to point down at the ice during the spin.

Sharpen Your Skills:
Practice left forward outside spirals to improve your flexibility and learn the camel spin position.

When you can do a camel spin with your arms extended to your sides, experiment with different arm positions. For example, try spinning with your left arm extended forward and your right arm extended above your right thigh, making a line from your left fingers to your right toe.

INTRODUCTION TO JUMPS

In free skating, there are two families of jumps: edge jumps and toe jumps.

Edge jumps spring from one foot gliding on an edge. The waltz jump and axel are edge jumps which take off from an edge moving forward. The salchow and loop are edge jumps which take off from an edge moving backward.

Toe jumps are also known as vaulting jumps because the skater vaults into the air with the aid of a toe pick tapped into the ice. Toe jumps take off from an edge moving backward. The toe jumps described in this chapter are mazurka, toe loop, half flip, half lutz, flip and lutz.

As you learn to do the different jumps, you need to memorize whether the takeoff is forward or backward, from which edge and whether there is an assist from a toe pick. While the takeoffs vary, the landings of most jumps look the same.

The vast majority of skaters rotate counterclockwise in their jumps and spins. It is OK to rotate clockwise if that is more natural for you. Some of the best skaters in the world jump that way. (See Page 67 for tips on deciding which way you should rotate. Your jumps and spins should rotate in the same direction.) Only a few talented skaters are able to jump and spin well in both directions.

The step-by-step instructions in this book are written for skaters who jump counterclockwise. If you are a clockwise jumper, switch right and left in the instructions.

JUMP POSITIONS
To perform jumps well, it is important that you understand correct body positions at various points of the jump.

Takeoff:
On the takeoff, your weight must be over the takeoff foot. The takeoff leg must be deeply bent to permit a strong spring. On a vaulting jump, a toe pick tapped on the ice helps the takeoff leg lift you into the air.

Your arms and upper body are as important as your legs when jumping. When preparing for takeoff, your arms should be extended and your shoulders and upper body checked, so they don't rotate before takeoff.

To lift off the ice, drop your arms slightly and then lift your arms to shoulder height. Then pull in your arms toward the center of your chest.

Lifting your arms helps to lift your upper body. But be careful not to raise or hunch your shoulders. Also, avoid throwing your arms around your body; swinging your arms in a circle will not help you rotate, it will make you lose control. Don't worry about getting enough rotation; the problem is controlling it. You should concentrate on lift rather than rotation.

In the air:

At the top of the jump, where most of the rotation occurs, your body rotates on a vertical axis, a line that runs from your head, down the center of your body. If your body leans too far in any direction — tilting or bending the vertical axis — the jump is likely to end in a fall.

In any jump that rotates more than180 degrees (loop, flip, lutz, axel), your body should rotate in the Standard Rotating Position:

Hold your left leg in front of your right, which will become the landing leg. Also, while rotating, cross your wrists in front of your chest and hold your elbows down, close to your sides.

(Later, if you attempt double and triple jumps, you will hold your legs closer together in the air and crossed at the ankles. This tighter position — called the reverse position — will keep your feet from separating due to centrifugal force.)

Landing:

With the exception of a few jumps that land forward, jumps look the same on landing: You glide on a right back outside edge with your right knee deeply bent and your arms extended to your sides. We call this the Standard Landing Position. The Standard Landing Position is first used on the waltz jump, and later on the toe loop, salchow, loop, flip, lutz and axel.

Landing — starting to push left leg back.

Standard Landing Position — gliding on RBO edge.

To achieve the Standard Landing Position, you must simultaneously extend your arms and free leg to check (or stop) your rotation.

On the way down from the top of the jump, push your left leg back. As you glide on the RBO edge, extend your left leg slightly outside the circle created by the RBO edge, rather than directly behind the skating foot or in the circle. Imagine landing on railroad tracks going around a curve: Your skating foot (right) glides on the inner rail, and your free leg (left) is held over the outer rail.

Your free leg (left) should be straight and open, with the knee turned out. The left toe should be turned out and pointed. Do not let your toe dangle or point down at the ice. Hold your free leg as high as possible without forcing your upper body to tip forward.

As you extend your left leg, also extend your arms strongly to your sides at shoulder height to check. Remember: On the takeoff, you pull in your arms to create rotation; on the landing, you check your arms to stop the rotation.

When you land, hold your shoulders and hips square to the circle on which you are skating on the RBO edge. Hold your head up, looking in the direction you came from, not where you are going.

Common errors on landings:
1. Free leg too high and chest too low. Corrections: Don't lean too far forward on the takeoff. Concentrate on holding up your chest and head when you land.
2. Allowing arms to drop on landing. Correction: Extend arms at shoulder level.
3. Overrotation on the landing, with your head, shoulders and free leg opening to the left. The landing edge makes a small circle instead of large curve. Corrections: Avoid overrotating on the takeoff. As you land, press your right shoulder back slightly while you glide backward. If overrotation is extreme, hold your left arm and shoulder more to the front than to the side. Look in the direction you came from, not over your left shoulder. Remember, the problem isn't creating rotation, it's controlling rotation.

TIMING

Skaters who want to perform jumps well must develop a good sense of timing. Each jump has its own particular rhythm. And because no two people have exactly the same combination of muscle fibers, timing can vary from one good jumper to another

The strength, endurance and flexibility of the muscles used in jumping can be improved with weight training, aerobic exercises and a stretching program. Both the upper- and lower-body muscle groups must be trained to work efficiently for correct jump execution.

Timing on edge jumps:

Compression and expansion — bending and straightening — of the jumping leg are necessary for strong spring. Compression occurs when the skater steps onto the jumping leg and bends the knee. The knee should be bent until the leg forms a 90 degree angle.

Expansion occurs when the skater jumps, straightening the skating leg and pushing off so the toe is the last part of the blade to leave the ice.

The timing on an edge jump can be counted: 1, 2 and 3, 4:
1. Step
2. Compress and
3. Spring
4. Land

Timing on toe jumps:

On a vaulting (toe) jump, the vault occurs when one leg is extended behind and the toe pick is tapped into the ice. If the picking leg is held firmly, the skater can ride into the air, like a pole vaulter rides a pole.

Like edge jumps, toe jumps require compression and expansion. The compression and expansion occur in the preparation leg, not the vaulting leg.

The timing on toe jumps can be counted: 1, 2, 3, 4.
1. Step
2. Turn and compress
3. Pick to vault (and expansion of the preparation leg)
4. Land

INSTRUCTIONS

The step-by-step instructions for each jump include the preparation, takeoff, body positions in the air, and landing. Timing is also discussed. Following the instructions for each jump is a list of common errors. The Sharpen Your Skills notes include exercises to help you learn the jump or ways to improve your performance.

Each jump can be entered several different ways. For each jump we describe preparatory steps that have worked well for our students. Your instructor may suggest other methods.

The jumps in this chapter are explained in order from easiest to most difficult. For safe, steady progress, make sure you can do one jump well before trying to learn the next one. Use the checklist at the end of this chapter to record your progress. The checklist also includes spins, because you need to learn spins along with jumps to be a complete free skater.

BUNNY HOP

Description:
  The bunny hop is the first jump most skaters learn. It has a forward takeoff and requires no rotation.

Left forward takeoff

Left forward landing

Right toe pick

Preparation:
  1. Glide forward on two feet.
  2. Lift your right foot and glide forward on your left foot.

Takeoff:
  1. Swing your right leg forward and swing your left arm forward.
  2. At the same time, spring off your left foot.

Landing:
  1. Land on your right toe pick.
  2. Immediately push from your right toe to your left foot and glide forward. Swing your right arm forward as you glide.

Common errors:
  1. Bending your right knee too much as you swing your right leg forward on the takeoff.
  2. Landing flat on the right blade, rather than on the toe pick.

Sharpen Your Skills:

Try doing a bunny hop with your left foot swinging forward instead of your right foot. Change the lefts and rights in the instructions.

As soon as you land one bunny hop, do another, and another.

Work on arm action to make your bunny hops bigger. As you do the series of bunny hops, swing your arms in a scissor motion: Swing your left arm forward as you swing your right leg forward on the takeoff. Swing your right arm forward as you land. This action should feel natural because it's the same arm movement used in walking or running.

takeoff

in the air

landing

landing

MAZURKA

Description:
 A mazurka is a small jump used to connect steps or jumps. There are many variations in foot and arm positions. Here, we describe one of the easiest ways to do a mazurka, starting from a standstill. Generally, the preparation and takeoff edge for a mazurka is a right back outside edge.

Preparation:
 1. Stand and hold your arms out to your sides.
 2. Look over your left shoulder.

Takeoff:
 1. Extend your left leg sideways, strike the ice with the left toe pick and spring into the air.

In the air:
 1. As you move to your left, bring your feet together in the air, touching right foot to left foot. This will feel like a gallop step to the side.

Landing:
 1. Land on the right toe pick.
 2. Immediately push to the left forward outside edge and glide. (This landing is similar to the bunny hop landing.)
 3. Continue to hold your left arm in front and your right arm behind — the same position as on the preparation.

Common errors:
 1. Facing forward, rather than sideways, when picking.

Sharpen Your Skills:
To get the feel for springing from and landing on your toe pick, try walking sideways on your picks.

When you can do a mazurka from a standstill, try gliding on a right back outside edge and, without stopping, do a mazurka.

Mazurka

takeoff

in the air

landing
step 1

landing
step 2

WALTZ JUMP

Description:
 The waltz jump is a half-revolution jump that takes off from the left forward outside edge, rotates counterclockwise, and lands on the right back outside edge. When the waltz jump is done well, it is a high, open, flowing jump. The waltz jump is used by many skaters as a warm up at every practice session. It is a precurser to the more difficult axel.

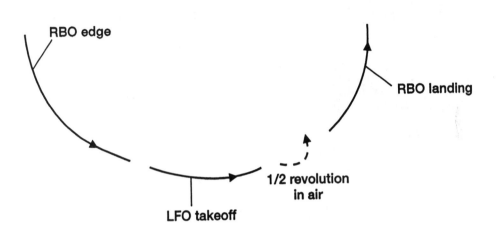

Preparation:
 1. Do back crossovers counterclockwise on a large circle.
 2. Glide on the right back outside edge and extend your left leg behind.
 3. Pass your arms close by your body and extend your left arm back, holding your left hand over your left foot. Hold your right arm in front over the circle.
 4. Look over your left shoulder.

Takeoff:
 1. Step onto the left forward outside edge with your left knee deeply bent. Keep your hips and shoulders square to the circle on which you are gliding. At the same time, reach back, behind your hips, with both hands.
 2. Spring from your left knee, pressing off the front of the blade. At the same time, pass your right leg and both arms forward.

In the air:
 1. Turn a half revolution counterclockwise with your legs extended as much as possible.
 2. As you turn, extend your arms in front of your chest, allowing your hands to meet.
 3. Hold your upper body straight up and down and face into the circle as you prepare to land.

Landing:
Land in the Standard Landing Position (Page 84).
1. Land on your right foot and glide backward on a right back outside edge with your knee deeply bent. As your right foot touches down, push your left leg back and extend it slightly outside the curve created by the RBO edge. Your left leg should be straight and open, with the knee turned out and the toe turned out and pointed.
2. As you extend your left leg, also check out with your arms; extending them strongly to your sides at shoulder height.
3. As you glide backward, hold your shoulders and hips square to the RBO curve. Hold your head up, looking in the direction you came from, not where you are going.

Timing: Count 1, 2 and 3, 4
1. Step on the LFO edge.
2. Compress left knee and
3. Spring.
4. Land on RBO edge.

Common errors:
1. Swinging your free leg and arms around your body, instead of straight forward, on the takeoff.
2. Not checking on the landing, allowing your left arm, shoulder, hip and leg to swing around to the left.
3. On the landing, allowing your left toe to dangle or point down at the ice.

Sharpen Your Skills:

Your first waltz jumps likely will be small and slow. You may even want to start from a standstill instead of back crossovers. Simply step from your left foot (moving forward) to your right foot (moving backward) to get the feel for this jump. Practice stepping over one of the hockey lines painted on the ice.

When you can step this jump with confidence, prepare for it with back crossovers as described in the instructions above. Gradually add speed to the back crossovers and spring more energetically from your left knee and lift with more power with your arms and right leg. Gradually, your waltz jump will gain height and distance.

On the landing, hold your left (free) leg as high and open as possible without forcing your upper body to tip forward. It will help to deeply bend your right knee as you land and glide backward.

Waltz Jump

preparation

takeoff

takeoff

landing

TOE LOOP

Description:
The toe loop is a one-revolution vaulting jump that takes off from the right back outside edge with a left-toe assist, rotates counterclockwise, and lands on the right back outside edge.

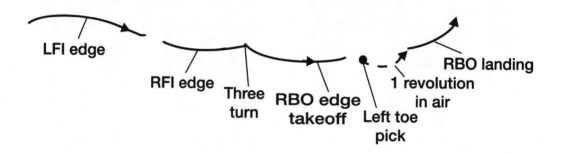

Preparation:
1. Skate forward and glide on a very shallow left forward inside edge. Hold your right foot low and pointed in front.
2. With your right arm in front and left arm behind, do a right forward inside three turn.

Takeoff:
1. Glide on the right back outside edge with a deeply bent knee. Extend your left leg straight behind. Also, after the three turn, check your arms: hold your left arm in front and your right arm behind. Look forward, toward your left hand.
2. Place the left toe pick in the ice and vault into the air. At the same time, lift up with your right foot.
3. Turning to the left, bring your right arm and leg in toward your body and then pass them forward, as in the waltz jump.

In the air:
Your position in the air will be the same as in the waltz jump.
1. Turn a half revolution counterclockwise with your right leg extended as much as possible.
2. Hold your arms in front of your chest, allowing your hands to meet.
3. Hold your upper body straight up and down and face into the circle as you prepare to land.

Landing:
Standard Landing Position.

Timing: Count to 4
1. Step on the RFI edge (entry of three turn).
2. Turn and compress right knee on RBO edge (exit of three turn).
3. Pick to vault.
4. Land on RBO edge.

Common errors:
1. Rotating your upper body and head to the left too early before takeoff, causing overrotation.
2. Turning on the left toe pick so the takeoff is forward instead of backward. These "toe waltz jumps" should be avoided.
3. Letting the left leg swing too far around (behind right leg) and into the circle before picking.
4. Bending the left knee and banging the toe pick on the ice when vaulting.

Sharpen Your Skills:
Work on keeping the vaulting leg (left) straight before placing the left toe pick on the ice. Make certain you bend your right knee as you reach back to pick with your left toe.

When you can do a waltz jump and a toe loop, you're ready to connect them in a jump combination. Use the landing edge of the waltz jump as the takeoff edge for the toe loop. Immediately after landing the waltz jump, pick with your left toe and do a toe loop. Note: There is no need to do a right forward inside three turn before the toe loop in this combination. Land the waltz jump with your left arm in front and your right arm behind to be ready for the toe loop takeoff. Land the toe loop in the Standard Landing Position.

Toe Loop

preparation, step 2   takeoff, step 1   takeoff, step 2

in the air   landing

HALF FLIP

Description:

A half flip is a half-revolution vaulting jump that takes off from the left back inside edge with a toe-pick assist, rotates counterclockwise and lands forward. The preparation for a half flip or flip may be either a mohawk or a three turn; a mohawk is used in these instructions.

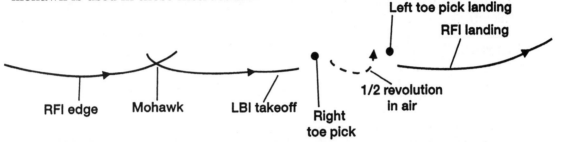

Preparation:
1. Skate forward and glide on your left foot. Hold your right foot low and pointed in front.
2. With your right arm in front, step to a very shallow right inside edge.
3. Do a right inside mohawk on a straight line.

Takeoff:
1. Coming out of the mohawk, glide backward on your left foot in a straight line. Hold your left arm in front and your right arm checked behind, over your right leg.
2. As you deeply bend your left knee, extend your right leg straight back and close to the ice.
3. Place your right toe pick in the ice and vault. Simultaneously lift up with your left leg and draw both arms toward your chest.

In the air:

Turn a half revolution counterclockwise.

Landing:
1. Land forward on your left toe pick.
2. Immediately push to your right foot and glide forward. Extend your left leg behind.
3. Check as you come down by extending your arms to your sides, with your left slightly in front.

Timing: Count to 4
1. Step on the RFI edge (entry to mohawk).
2. Turn and bend your knee as you glide backward (exit of mohawk).
3. Pick to vault.
4. Land forward.

Common errors:
1. Curving too much on the mohawk in the preparation, which makes rotation difficult to control.
2. Failing to bend your left knee while gliding backward before the takeoff, resulting in a small jump.
3. Picking too close to the left foot or picking too far to the right, resulting in a small jump.
4. Lifting the right foot too high before placing the toe pick on the ice for the takeoff.

Sharpen Your Skills:

Prepare for a half flip with a LFO three turn instead of a right mohawk. Make sure the LFO three turn follows a straight line rather than a curve.

Try several half flips in a row. As soon as you land one, do a mohawk and take off again.

---

preparation
step 2

takeoff
step 3

landing
step 2

HALF LUTZ

Description:

A half lutz is a half-revolution vaulting jump that takes off from the left back outside edge with a toe-pick assist, rotates counterclockwise and lands forward. Note that the half flip and half lutz (and the flip and lutz) have similar takeoffs — only the back edge is different. The flip takes off from the left back inside edge and the lutz takes off from the left back outside edge.

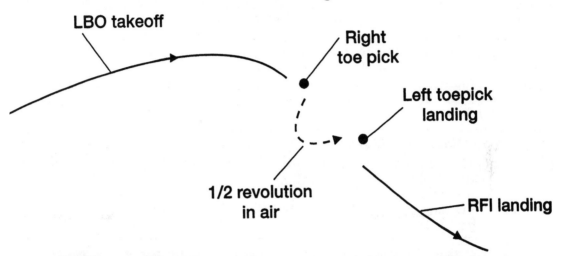

Preparation:

1. Do backward crossovers clockwise on a large circle. (This is opposite the direction of the preparation for a waltz jump.)
2. Maintaining a shallow curve, glide on the left back outside edge. Hold your right foot at your left heel.
3. Move your arms, so your left arm is in front and your right arm is in back. Look forward, toward your left hand.

Takeoff:

1. Deeply bend your left knee and extend your right leg straight back. Continue to reach back with your right hand.
2. Place the right toe pick in the ice and vault. Simultaneously lift up with your left leg and draw both arms toward your chest.

In the air:

Turn a half revolution counterclockwise.

Landing:

This landing is the same as for a half flip:

1. Land forward on your left toe pick.
2. Immediately push to your right foot and glide forward. Extend your left leg behind.
3. Check as you come down by extending your arms to your sides, with your left slightly in front.

Timing: Count to 4
1. Glide on the LBO edge.
2. Compress your left knee.
3. Pick to vault.
4. Land forward.

Common errors:
1. Dropping your right side on the takeoff. This puts you on the left back inside edge, which makes the jump a half flip instead of a half lutz.
2. Not picking straight behind or planting the toe pick too close to the skating foot. These errors cause the jump to be small.
3. On the landing, gliding on the right forward outside edge (instead of a shallow RFI edge). A half lutz follows an S-shaped pattern; the takeoff and landing create different curves.

Sharpen Your Skills:

Try a half lutz/half flip combination. After you land the half lutz (gliding on your right foot), do a mohawk for the half flip.

Try a half lutz/toe loop combination. Land the half lutz and go right into a RFI three turn for the toe loop.

preparation

takeoff

in the air

landing

SALCHOW

Description:
  The salchow is a one-revolution edge jump that takes off from the left back inside edge, rotates counterclockwise, and lands on the right back outside edge.

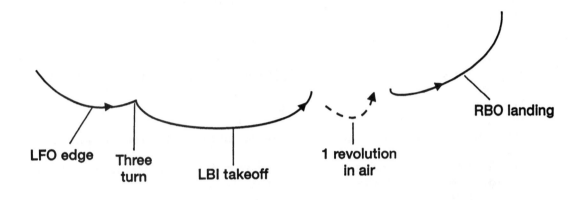

LFO edge   Three turn   LBI takeoff   1 revolution in air   RBO landing

Preparation:
  The first four steps of the preparation are the same as for the waltz jump.
  1. Do back crossovers counterclockwise on a large circle.
  2. Glide on the right back outside edge and extend your left leg behind.
  3. Pass your arms close by your body and extend your left arm back. Hold your left hand above your left foot. Hold your right arm in front over the circle.
  4. Look back over your left shoulder.
  5. Step forward onto left forward outside edge and do a LFO three turn with your right leg extended directly back from your right hip.

Takeoff:
  1. Glide on the left back inside edge with a deeply bent left knee. Check, holding your right arm and leg back. Hold your left arm in front over the circle. Look forward, toward your left hand.
  2. Release your right arm and leg, allowing them to draw in toward your body. Bend your left knee even more.
  3. Spring from the left back inside edge, pressing off the front of the blade. Simultaneously, reach through with your right arm and leg, as in the waltz jump.

In the air:
  In the air, the salchow feels like the waltz jump and the toe loop.
  1. Turn a half revolution counterclockwise as you continue to extend your right leg.
  2. Lift with both arms and hold them in front of your chest.
  3. Hold your upper body straight up and down and face into the circle as you prepare to land.

Landing:
Standard Landing Position.

Timing: Count 1, 2 and, 3, 4
1. Step on the LFO edge (entry to three turn).
2. Turn, bend left knee, glide on the LBI edge (exit of three turn) and
3. Spring.
4. Land on RBO edge.

Common errors:
1. Bending forward from your waist and letting your upper body, arms and head lean out of the circle (to the left) on the takeoff.
2. Arms and free leg rotating and lifting at different times, instead of simultaneously.
3. Dropping your right arm and right side on the takeoff, creating an uneven lifting motion.
4. Spinning on the takeoff; not checking your right shoulder, hip and free leg while on the RBI edge after the three turn.
5. Pulling in the right knee too close to the skating leg on the takeoff. Or letting the free leg swing too wide.

Sharpen Your Skills:

Your first few attempts at the salchow can be done slowly, without a back-crossover preparation. From a standstill, push into a LFO three turn and continue with the instructions for the takeoff.

Check the print on the ice after doing a salchow. The LBI edge coming out of the three turn should be about twice as long as the LFO edge entering the three turn.

Instead of entering a salchow from a LFO three turn, try doing a right inside mohawk. The step coming out of the mohawk will be a LBI edge, the correct takeoff edge. Checking the shoulders and free leg while on the LBI edge is vital.

Salchow

preparation, step 5

takeoff, step 1

takeoff, step 3

in the air

landing

LOOP

Description:
A loop is a one-revolution jump that takes off from the right back outside edge, rotates counterclockwise, and lands on the right back outside edge. Skaters use many different preparations for this jump. Two preparations are explained here.

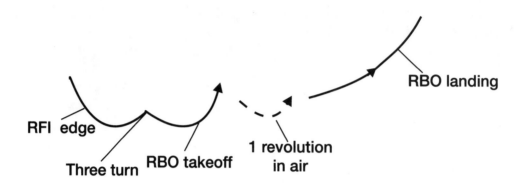

RFI edge

Three turn   RBO takeoff

1 revolution
in air

RBO landing

Preparation 1:
1. Glide forward on your left foot.
2. Step to your right foot with your right arm in front and do a right inside three turn on a small circle.
3. Immediately after the turn (you will be on the right back outside edge), hold your left leg and left arm in front of your body, over the circle. Strongly check your shoulders, holding your right arm behind. Look forward, toward your left hand.

Takeoff 1:
1. Immediately after the turn, bend your right knee deeply, allowing the RBO edge to curve into the circle.
2. Spring from the RBO edge, pressing off the front of the blade. As you spring, draw your left hand in toward your chest and release your shoulders to square off your hips. Also, bring your right hand to your chest.

Preparation 2:
1. Do a left forward outside three turn.
2. Step to your right foot and glide on the right back outside edge with your right knee deeply bent. Lightly rest your left foot on the ice in front of your right foot and slightly out of the circle. Note: All of your weight will be over your right foot.
3. Strongly check your shoulders, holding your left arm in front and your right arm behind. Look forward, toward your left hand.

Takeoff 2:
1. Bend your right knee more deeply, allowing the RBO edge to curve into the circle.
2. Spring from the RBO, pressing off the front of the right blade. Lift your left leg in front.
3. As you spring, lift your arms and draw both hands toward your chest.

In the air:
Turn one revolution counterclockwise in the Standard Rotating Position.
1. Hold your left leg in front of your right (which will become the landing leg).
2. While rotating, cross your wrists in front of your chest and hold your elbows down, close to your sides.

Landing:
Standard Landing Position.

Timing: (Using Preparation 1) Count 1, 2 and, 3, 4
1. Step on RFI edge (entry to three turn)
2. Turn, compress your knee on RBO edge (exit of three turn) and
3. Spring.
4. Land on RBO edge.

Common errors:
1. Allowing your shoulders to rotate too early and letting your upper body lean outside the circle before takeoff.
2. Letting your left leg drift behind your right leg before the takeoff. The left leg should stay in front of the right leg until the landing.

Sharpen Your Skills:
When you can do a loop jump easily, try doing two in a row. As you land the first loop, check strongly with your arms and shoulders and keep your left leg in front, rather than extending it behind; this is the takeoff position required for the second loop. Land the second loop in the Standard Landing Position.

Loop

preparation 1, step 2

preparation 1, step 3

takeoff 1, step 2

landing

landing

takeoff 2, step 1

preparation 2, step 2

FLIP

Description:
   A flip is a one-revolution vaulting jump that takes off from the left back inside edge with a toe-pick assist, rotates counterclockwise and lands on the right back outside edge. The preparation and takeoff are the same as for a half flip.

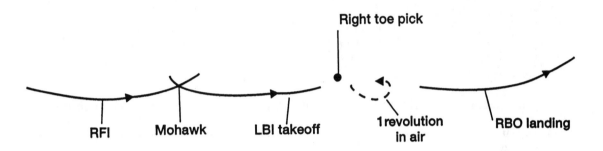

Preparation:
   1. Skate forward and glide on your left foot. Hold your right foot low and pointed in front.
   2. With your right arm in front, step to a right inside edge.
   3. Do a RFI mohawk on a straight line.

Takeoff:
   1. Coming out of the mohawk, glide backward on your left foot in a straight line. Hold your left arm in front and your right arm checked behind, over your right leg.
   2. As you deeply bend your left knee, extend your right leg straight back and close to the ice.
   3. Place the right toe pick in the ice and vault. Simultaneously lift up with your left leg and draw both arms toward your chest.

In the air:
   Turn one revolution counterclockwise in the Standard Rotating Position.

Landing:
   Standard Landing Position.

Timing: Count to 4
   1. Step on the RFI edge (entry to mohawk).
   2. Turn and compress your left knee as you glide backward (exit of mohawk).
   3. Pick to vault.
   4. Land on RBO edge.

Common errors:
1. Curving too much on the mohawk in the preparation. Too much curve makes it difficult to control rotation.
2. Failing to bend your left knee while gliding backward before the takeoff, resulting in a small jump.
3. Picking too close to the left foot or picking too far to the right, resulting in a small jump.

Sharpen Your Skills:

Prepare for a flip with a three turn instead of a mohawk. Glide forward on your left foot and use your right toe to push yourself into a LFO three. Make the three turn as straight as possible and strongly check your shoulders after the turn as you glide backward on your left foot. Vault and land as instructed above.

When you can land a flip with confidence, try a flip/toe loop or flip/loop combination.

Flip

preparation, step 2

takeoff, step 3

in the air

landing

LUTZ

Description:
A lutz is a one-revolution vaulting jump that takes off from the left back outside edge with a toe-pick assist, rotates counterclockwise and lands on the right backward outside edge. Review half lutz, page 99.

A lutz is one of the easiest jumps to identify because of the distinctive preparation. Skaters typically do back crossovers and glide backward into a corner to do a lutz.

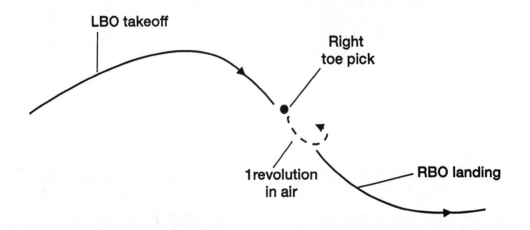

Preparation:
1. Do backward crossovers clockwise on a large circle.
2. Maintaining a shallow curve, glide on the left back outside edge. Hold your right foot at your left heel.
3. Move your arms, so your left arm is in front and your right arm is in back. Look forward, toward your left hand.

Takeoff:
1. Deeply bend your left knee and extend your right leg straight back. Continue to reach back with your right hand.
2. Place the right toe pick in the ice and vault. Simultaneously lift up with your left leg and draw both arms toward your chest.

In the air:
Do one revolution counterclockwise in the Standard Rotating Position.

Landing:
Standard Landing Position.

Timing: Count to 4
1. Glide on the LBO edge.
2. Compress your left knee.
3. Pick to vault.
4. Land.

Common Errors:
1. Looking down and pressing your left hand down on the takeoff, which **causes** your body to tilt in the air.
2. Dropping your right side on the takeoff. This puts you on a left back **inside** edge, which makes the jump a flip instead of a lutz — call it a "flutz."
3. Pressing your right arm too far around and behind before the takeoff.
4. Picking somewhere other than straight behind or planting the toe **pick too** close to the skating foot, causing the jump to be small.

Sharpen Your Skills:

A good jump will have as much speed on the landing as on the takeoff. Make sure you don't scratch to a halt on your landing.

When you can land a lutz with confidence, use it in a combination: lutz/toe loop or lutz/loop.

takeoff, step 1

takeoff, step 2

in the air

landing

AXEL

Description:
Axels (single, double and triple) are the only major jumps that take off forward. Because of the forward takeoff, the single axel requires 1 1/2 revolutions, a half turn more than other single jumps, so it can be landed backward. The axel takes off from the left forward outside edge, rotates 1 1/2 turns counterclockwise and lands on the right back outside edge.

Some skaters consider the axel the king of jumps because it can be performed with such speed, height and distance that it seems to float through the air.

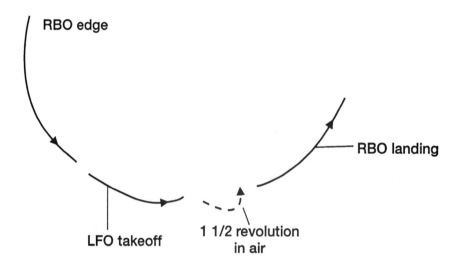

RBO edge

RBO landing

LFO takeoff

1 1/2 revolution
in air

Preparation:
The preparation for an axel is the same as for a waltz jump:
1. Do back crossovers counterclockwise on a large circle.
2. Glide on a right back outside edge and extend your left leg behind.
3. Pass your arms close by your body and extend your left arm back, holding left hand over left foot. Hold your right arm in front over the circle.
4. Look over your left shoulder.

Takeoff:
1. Step onto a left forward outside edge with your left knee deeply bent. Keep your hips and shoulders square to the circle on which you are gliding. With your upper body, lean forward slightly over your left foot. Reach back, behind your hips, with both hands. Look straight ahead and keep your chin up.
2. Spring from your left knee, pressing off the front of the blade. At the same time, swing your right leg forward (as if running up three steps) and lift with both arms.

In the air:
Turn 1 1/2 revolutions counterclockwise in the Standard Rotating Position.

As in other jumps, most of the rotation occurs at the top of the jump's arc. In an axel, it is especially important to keep your body straight and vertical while rotating.

Landing:
Standard Landing Position.

Timing: Count 1, 2 and.3, 4
1. Step on the LFO edge.
2. Compress your left knee and
3. Spring.
4. Land on RBO edge.

Common errors:
1. Rotating on the ice on the LFO edge before taking off.
2. Jumping in the "flamingo" position, the result of rotating too quickly on the takeoff and not passing the free leg forward.
3. Wrapping your left leg around your right, rather than lifting your left leg just before landing.

Sharpen Your Skills:
Here are some exercises that may prepare you to attempt an axel:
1. Practice a waltz jump/loop jump combination.
2. Practice doing a back spin on the landing of a waltz jump.
3. Practice axels on the floor in your shoes to get used to the rotation.

Some skaters use this preparation for their first attempts at an axel: 1. Skate a right forward outside edge. 2. Step to the left forward outside edge with your arms behind your hips. 3. Take off.

Axel

preparation,
steps 3, 4

takeoff,
step 1

takeoff,
step 2

in the air

landing

landing

Chapter 4 Free Skating Checklist

The Free Skating chapter includes the following skills, including basic maneuvers, spins and jumps. If you want to be a complete and balanced skater, you need to learn jumps and spins simultaneously. So, jumps and spins are combined on this list in order of difficulty. (The page numbers indicate where to find the instructions in Chapter 4.)

When you have mastered one skill, check it off and move on to the next skill on the list. To make safe and steady progress, make sure you can do the skills in one section (beginning, intermediate or advanced) before you attempt the more difficult skills in the next section.

Chapter 5
Figures

*F*igures are alive and well, despite the misperception that skaters don't do them anymore. It's only at the top levels of international competition that figures have been eliminated. In the United States, one national champion is chosen in figures and another in free skating.

Many skaters, beginning and advanced, still practice and enjoy figures. You can too.

Many coaches encourage their skating students to learn figures, which are also known as "compulsory figures" and "school figures." Like the scales practiced over and over by a piano player, figures teach fundamentals of figure skating.

The edges you learned in the Basics chapter will be used in edge exercises and figures in this chapter.

You will start by learning to do edges along an axis. Step-by-step instructions will help you do exercises with forward outside edges, forward inside edges, back outside edges and back inside edges.

This chapter also includes instructions for doing the four basic figure eights: forward outside, forward inside, back outside and back inside.

Use the Figures Checklist to record your progress in learning figures.

As you get started on figures, let's review the abbreviations commonly used when discussing edges and figures:

RFO: Right Forward Outside
LFO: Left Forward Outside
RFI: Right Forward Inside
LFI: Left Forward Inside
RBO: Right Back Outside
LBO: Left Back Outside
RBI: Right Back Inside
LBI: Left Back Inside

EDGES: GLIDING AND LEANING

Learning and perfecting figures develops the skill of gliding. Without learning to glide well, a skater never discovers the true fun of skating.

Skating blades glide in two directions, forward and backward.

The bottom of each blade is concave, so it has two edges. One edge is the inside edge, the other is the outside edge. When skating on an edge, the blade glides on a curve. To skate on an edge, both the skater and the blade must lean into the curve. The body lean should match the blade lean. The amount of lean depends on the amount of speed and the size of the curve. An edge is considered "shallow" if the curve is relatively flat. An edge is "deep" if the curve is round.

When doing figures, it is important that you stand as tall and straight as possible. This presses your weight directly on your skating foot. The pressure — from your weight and the friction of the blade on the ice — melts the top layer of ice, reducing it to water. Water is the lubricant that allows the blade to glide on the ice.

After you learn the four basic eights, you may learn many variations. In some more-advanced figures, three turns and other turns are added at various points on the circle. The figures known as "serpentines" have three circles instead of two. The figures known as "loops" consist of small circles with teardrop-shaped loops drawn inside. The USFSA *Rulebook* contains diagrams for all the compulsory figures.

As in free skating and ice dancing, members of the USFSA and ISIA may take a series of proficiency tests in figures. The USFSA program includes nine tests, from Preliminary through Senior. ISIA members may take 10 Figure Skating tests.

Edge exercises

You were introduced to edges in Chapter 3 Basics. In this chapter, you will learn exercises to sharpen your edge skills. These exercises will help you practice all the edges: right and left, forward and backward, inside and outside.

In these edge exercises, you will learn to skate a series of edges across the width of the rink. You will skate a semicircle on each edge, first on your right foot and then on your left, along a line known as the long axis. At first, it's best to do the edge exercises along an axis you can see, such as one of the hockey lines painted on the ice. Later you can place edges along an invisible axis.

Edge exercises will help you learn to make transitions from one foot to the other and to rotate your arms, shoulders and hips correctly. After mastering edges, you can apply your skills to figure eights.

Here are some tips that apply to all the edge exercises:

1. Keep your body and skating blade as still as possible as you glide. Every wiggle will slow you down and distort the circle.
2. Move only one part of your body at a time. For example, move your free foot, then your arms. To control rotation, move slowly and carefully.
3. When your arms move, they should pass close to your body, rather than rotating wide around your body in a horizontal motion.
4. Hold your palms facing down, as if pressing on a table.
5. Bend your knees for every pushoff. After each pushoff, rise on your skating knee. Skate the edge on a slightly bent knee.
6. Use your inside edge, not the toe pick, when you push off.

REMINDER: When discussing backward skills, remember that when your arm is in "front," it is in front of your upper body. When your arm is in "back," or "behind," it is behind your back.

FORWARD OUTSIDE EDGES

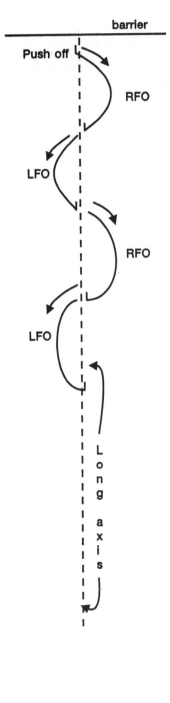

Skate semicircles, alternating RFO and LFO edges, along an axis the width of the rink.

1. Stand on the long axis with your left side nearest the barrier. Place your feet in a T position, with your left toe pointing to the barrier. Hold your right arm in front and your left arm behind. Bend your knees and push to the RFO edge. Look in the direction your skating toe is pointing.
2. Glide on the RFO edge. Continue to hold your right arm in front and your left arm behind. Bring your left toe to your right heel. Rise on your right knee.
3. Pass your left foot forward and point your toe, holding it over the curve. Then slowly pass your arms close to your body until your left arm is in front and your right arm is behind.
4. As you approach the line, bring your feet together, holding your left foot just above the ice. Bend your knees, press your right blade to the inside edge and push to the LFO edge.
5. Glide on the LFO edge. Continue to hold your left arm in front and your right arm behind. Bring your right toe to your left heel.
6. Pass your right foot forward and point your toe, holding it over the curve. Then slowly pass your arms close to your body until your right arm is in front and your left arm is behind.
7. Without stopping, make semicircles, alternating RFO and LFO edges as you move across the ice.

Sharpen Your Skills

Try this exercise on clean ice. Check the print to make certain all the semicircles are the same size and shape.

Make your movements slow and controlled.

As you move your free leg forward, don't let it swing wide, as if kicking a soccer ball. Also, don't rotate your arms wide around your body; your arms should pass close to your sides.

Make sure your body weight is on the back of the blade.

You should be able to do at least four semicircles, on alternating feet, across the width of the rink.

Forward Outside Edges

step 1

step 2

step 3

step 4

step 5

FORWARD INSIDE EDGES

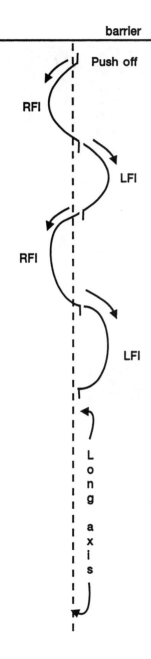

Skate semicircles, alternating RFI and LFI edges, along an axis the width of the rink.

1. Stand on the long axis with your right side near the barrier. Place your feet in a T position, with your left toe pointing down the long axis. Hold your left arm forward and your right arm to your side. Bend your knees and push to the RFI edge. Look in the direction your skating toe is pointing.
2. Glide on the RFI edge. Continue to hold your left arm in front and your right arm to your side. Bring your left toe to your right heel. Rise on your right knee.
3. Pass your left foot forward and point your toe, holding it over the curve. Then slowly pass your arms close to your body until your right arm is in front and your left arm is to your side.
4. As you approach the line, bring your feet together, holding your left foot just above the ice. Bend your knees and push to the LFI edge.
5. Glide on the LFI edge. Continue to hold your right arm in front and your left arm to your side. Bring your right toe to your left heel. Rise on your left knee.
6. Pass your right foot forward and point your toe, holding it over the curve. Then slowly pass your arms close to your body until your left arm is in front and your right arm is to your side.
7. Without stopping, make semicircles, alternating RFI and LFI edges as you move across the ice.

Sharpen Your Skills

Avoid pushing with your toe picks when making the transition from one foot to the other.

Keep your body weight over the back of the blade. Avoid lunging forward when you push.

Overrotation of the shoulders is a common problem on inside edges.

Keep your movements slow and controlled; don't let your arms swing around you.

Forward Inside Edges

step 1

step 2

step 3

step 4

step 5

BACK OUTSIDE EDGES

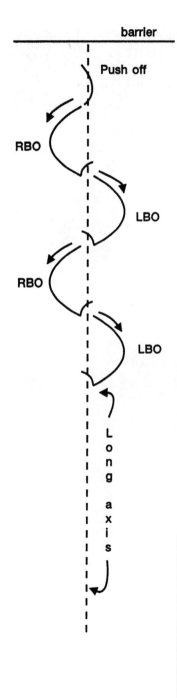

Skate semicircles, alternating RBO and LBO edges, along an axis the width of the rink.

1. Stand with your back to the barrier, feet about hip-width apart. Lift your right leg with your knee and toe pointed in. Then bend your left knee and push to the RBO edge with your right arm held back over the intended semicircle. Look into the semicircle.
2. Glide on the RBO edge with your right knee bent. Hold your left foot, with toe pointed, in front of the skating foot. Continue to hold your right arm back over the semicircle and left arm in front. Look into the semicircle. Rise on your right knee.
3. Pass your left toe back and hold it at your right heel. Next, pass your arms close to your body so your left arm is in back and your right arm is in front. Then turn your head to the left and look over your left shoulder toward the axis. Hold this position and glide to the axis.
4. At the axis, bend your right knee, press your right blade to the inside edge, and push to the LBO edge.
5. Glide on the LBO edge with your left knee bent. Hold your right foot, with toe pointed, in front of the skating foot. Hold your left arm back over the semicircle and right arm in front. Look into the semicircle. Rise on your left knee.
6. Pass your right toe back and hold it at your left heel. Next, pass your arms close to your body so your right arm is in back and your left arm is in front. Then turn your head to the right and look over your right shoulder toward the axis. Hold this position and glide to the axis.
7. Without stopping, make semicircles, alternating RBO and LBO edges, as you move across the ice.

Sharpen Your Skills
Just before the push, the skating foot must switch from the back outside edge to the back inside edge.

Avoid leaning out of the circle as you turn your head and shoulders.

Your body weight should be over the middle-front of the blade. If you hear scratching noises, you are too far forward.

Back Outside Edges

step 1

step 1

step 2

step 3

step 4

step 5

BACK INSIDE EDGES

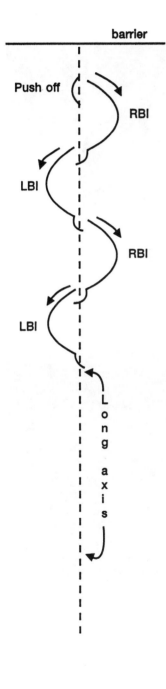

Skate semicircles, alternating RBI and LBI edges, along an axis the width of the rink.

1. Stand facing the barrier, with your feet about hip-width apart. Lift your right leg with your knee and toe pointed in. Then bend your left knee and push to the RBI edge. Extend your right arm to your side, pointing away from the axis. Hold your left arm in front and look into the semicircle.
2. Glide on the RBI edge with your knee bent. Hold your left foot, with toe pointed, in front of the skating foot. Continue to hold your right arm to your side, and your left foot and left hand in front, over the semicircle. Rise on your right knee.
3. Look over your left shoulder to see where you are going. Next, pass your left toe back and hold it at your right heel. Then slowly pass your arms close to your body until your left arm is behind and your right arm is in front. Hold this position and glide to the axis.
4. At the axis, bend your right knee and push to the LBI edge.
5. Glide on the LBI edge with your knee bent. Hold your right foot, with toe pointed, in front of the skating foot. Hold your left arm to your side, pointing away from the axis, and your right arm in front.
6. Look over your right shoulder to see where you are going. Next, pass your right toe back and hold it at your left heel. Then pass your arms close to your body until your right arm is to your side and your left arm is in front. Hold this position and glide to the axis.
7. Without stopping, make semicircles, alternating RBI and LBI edges, as you move across the ice.

Sharpen Your Skills

Your body weight should be over the middle-front of the blade. If you hear scratching noises, you are too far forward.

As you move the free foot past the skating foot, keep the free foot close enough to touch the skating foot. Balancing will be difficult if your foot swings wide or your free toe points into the semicircle.

Back Inside Edges

step 1

step 1

step 2

step 3

step 4

step 5

FOUR BASIC FIGURE EIGHTS

When you can do the edge exercises with some control, you're ready to try figure eights.

Figures are skated on circles arranged in the shape of the numeral 8. That's why they're called figure eights. All figures (except loop figures, which are much smaller) are based on four basic eights: forward outside, forward inside, back outside, back inside. When you master the basic eights, you will be able to glide with control on all eight edges. You will have a foundation for safe and secure skating.

Each figure eight consists of two circles that meet at a "center." Starting at the center, you will push once and glide around a large circle on your right foot. Without stopping at the center, you will push again and glide around the other circle on your left foot. Each circle can be skated as many times as you wish. With practice, you will be able to set up round circles and trace them.

Using a scribe

Many skaters use a scribe to draw circles on the ice when practicing figures. A scribe works like a compass used to draw circles on paper. A scribe consists of telescoping metal tubes that can be extended to the desired length. One end of the scribe is pushed into the ice at the center of the desired circle. When the scribe is rotated, a sharp point at the other end scratches a circle on the ice.

A scribe is used to draw circles on the ice.

Most beginning figure skaters find a scribe helpful when they practice the basic figure eights because it is difficult to create circles that are the right size and round. With the scribe, you can draw a perfect pattern and then try to trace it. By repetition of each figure, your body learns the rhythm of the movement and acquires muscle memory.

Tips for figures

Here are 10 principles that apply to the four basic eights:

1. Each circle should have a diameter three times your height. For example, a person who is 5 feet tall will skate a circle 15 feet in diameter. You may want to use a scribe until you get used to making a circle the appropriate size.
2. The two circles should be arranged so their centers are on an invisible line known as the long axis. The short axis is an imaginary line between the two circles, perpendicular to the long axis.
3. The center is where the two circles come together. Pushing and stepping correctly will help make the center neat and the circles round. The transition from one foot to the other must be done very carefully, like threading a needle.
4. Body position and erect posture are very important. Your shoulders "hold" the circle, which means they are parallel to the circle. Keep your hips square (on a line perpendicular) to the circle.
5. As you travel around the circle, move only one part of your body at a time. For example, move your free foot, then your arms. All movements should be slow and careful to help control rotation.
6. When you move your arms, they should pass in a pendulum-like motion close to your body, rather than rotating wide around your body in a horizontal motion.
7. Hold your palms facing down, as if pressing on a table.
8. Bend your knees for each pushoff. After pushing off, rise on the skating knee. Skate the figure on a slightly bent knee.
9. Use your inside edge, not the toe pick, when you push off.
10. Try to glide as smoothly as possible. Every wiggle will slow you down and distort the circle.

Diagrams

On the figure diagrams, each circle is divided in thirds and each one-third is labeled with a letter and a number, such as R1. R1 refers to the first one-third of the circle which is skated on the right foot. For each figure, the numbers in the instructions correspond to the numbers in the diagram. The instructions explain how to push off and what to do during each one-third of the circle.

In the following instructions, "center" refers to the center of the figure — where the two circles meet — rather than the center of the circle you are skating.

FORWARD OUTSIDE EIGHT

Draw two circles with a scribe. Or draw a line with your heel to mark the center.

One circle is skated on the RFO edge, the other on the LFO edge. Review Forward Outside Edges, page 119.

Start at the center: Stand in a T position, with your right arm in front and left arm behind. Push to the RFO edge.

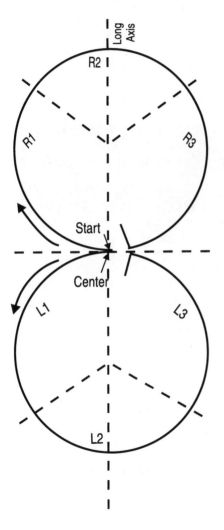

R1: Glide on the RFO edge with your right arm in front, left arm behind. Hold your left toe at your right heel. Rise on your right knee.

R2: Pass your left foot forward and point your toe, holding it over the circle. Then slowly pass your arms close to your body, until your left arm is in front and your right arm is behind. Look toward the center.

R3: Hold this position and glide to the center.

Center: Bring your feet together, holding your left foot just above the ice. Bend your knees, press your right blade to the inside edge, and push to the LFO edge to start the new circle.

L1: Glide on the LFO edge with your left arm in front, right arm behind. Hold your right toe at your left heel.

L2: Pass your right foot forward and point your toe, holding it over the circle. Then slowly pass your arms close to your body, until your right arm is in front and your left arm is behind. Look toward the center.

L3: Hold this position and glide to the center.

Repeat the RFO and LFO edge circles, trying to trace as closely as possible.

Forward Outside Eight

start at center   R1

R3   center, starting circle on left foot

Sharpen Your Skills:

At first you may not be able to make it all the way around a circle on one push. As you practice and learn to glide smoothly, you will accomplish this. It will help if you hold your body very still as you glide, moving your arms and free leg only at the appropriate points.

When you can trace scribed circles fairly well, try to do this figure on clean ice without drawing the figure first with a scribe.

FORWARD INSIDE EIGHT

Draw two circles with a scribe. Or draw a line with your heel to mark the center.

One circle is skated on the RFI edge, the other on the LFI edge. Review **Forward Inside Edges, page 121.**

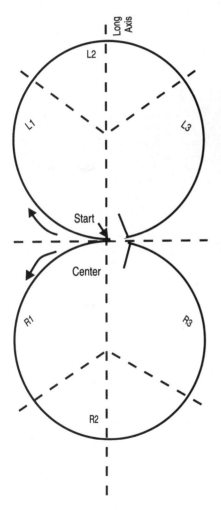

Start at the center: Stand in a T position, with your left arm in front and right arm to your side. Push to the RFI edge.

R1: Glide on the RFI edge with your left arm in front, right arm to your side. Hold your left toe at your right heel.

R2: Pass your left foot forward and point your toe, holding it over the circle. Then slowly pass your arms close to your body, until your right arm is in front and your left arm is to your side. Look toward the center.

R3: Hold this position and glide to the center.

Center: Bring your feet together, holding your left foot just above the ice. Bend your knees, turn your right toe toward the new circle, and push to the LFI edge to start the new circle.

L1: Glide on the LFI edge with your right arm in front and left arm to your side. Hold your right toe at your left heel.

L2: Pass your right foot forward and point your toe, holding it over the circle. Then slowly pass your arms close to your body, until your left arm is in front and your right arm is to your side.

L3: Hold this position and glide to the center.

Repeat the RFI and LFI circles, trying to trace as closely as possible.

　　　　　　Figure Skating

Forward Inside Eight

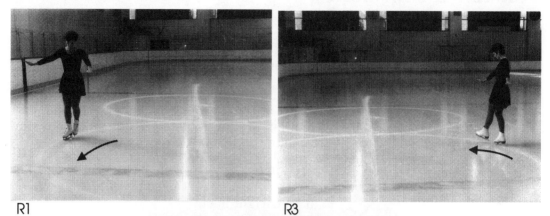

R1　　　　　　　　　　　　　　　R3

center, starting circle on left foot

Sharpen Your Skills:

Avoid using your toe picks when you push off between circles. This error is especially common on pushes from the inside edge on one foot to the inside edge on the other foot.

If your circles are wiggly, try standing up straighter and maintaining consistent lean into the circle. A little more speed will probably help.

Having trouble remembering which arm leads on eights and edges? Try this memory trick:

When skating inside edges and eights, start with the opposite arm. That is, when you are on your right foot, start with your left arm in front. Remember inside and opposite.

When skating outside edges and eights, start with the same arm. That is, start with your right arm in front when skating on your right foot. Remember outside and same.

BACK OUTSIDE EIGHT

Draw two circles with a scribe. Or draw a line with your heel to mark the center.

One circle is skated on the RBO edge, the other on the LBO edge. Review Back Outside Edges, page 123.

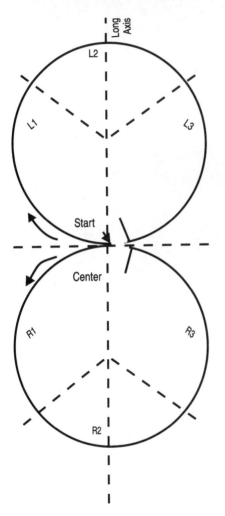

Start at the center: Stand with your feet about hip-width apart on the short axis, facing the circle you will skate first on your right foot. To push off, lift your right leg with your knee and toe pointed in. Bend your left knee and push to the RBO edge with your right arm back over the circle.

R1: Glide on the RBO edge with your right knee bent. Hold your left foot, with toe pointed, in front of the skating foot. Hold your right arm back over the circle and left arm in front of your body. Look into the circle. Rise on your right knee.

R2: Pass your left toe back and hold it at your right heel. Next, slowly pass your arms close to your body until your left arm is in back and your right arm is in front. Then turn your head to the left and look over your left shoulder toward the center.

R3: Hold this position and glide to the center.

Center: Bend your right knee, press your right blade to the inside edge, and push to the LFO edge, starting the new circle. Hold your left arm back over the circle. Look into the new circle.

L1: Glide on the LBO edge with your left knee bent. Hold your right foot, with toe pointed, in front of the skating foot. Hold your left arm back over the circle and right arm in front of your body. Look into the circle. Rise on your left knee.

L2: Pass your right toe back and hold it at your left heel. Next, slowly pass your arms close to your body until your right arm is in back and your left arm is in front. Then turn your head to the right and look over your right shoulder toward the center.

L3: Hold this position and glide to the center. Repeat the RBO and LBO circles, tracing as closely as possible.

Back Outside Eight

start at center

R1

R3

center, starting circle on left foot

Sharpen Your Skills

Be sure to keep your free leg in front of the skating foot after pushing to a new circle. Don't let your free leg swing wide, out of the circle.

The first pushoff is the most difficult. Make certain you turn your right hip and heel hard to the right so you can step down on the RBO edge.

Concentrate on making the center neat. Make sure the stepdowns and pushoffs aren't crisscrossed.

When trying to see the circle, look down with your eyes, not your entire upper body.

BACK INSIDE EIGHT

Draw two circles with a scribe. Or draw a line with your heel to mark the center.

One circle is skated on the RBI edge, the other on the LBI edge. Review Back Inside Edges, page 125.

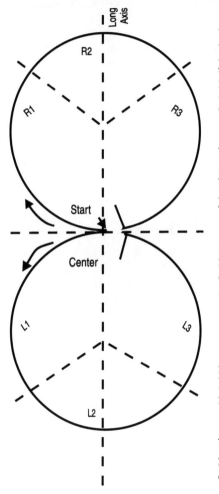

Start at the center: Stand with your feet hip-width apart on the short axis and with your back to the circle you will skate first. To push off, lift your right leg with your knee and toe pointed in. Bend your left knee and push to the RBI edge. Extend your right arm to your side, pointing out of the circle. Look into the circle.

R1: Glide on the RBI edge with your right knee bent. Continue to hold your right arm to your side and your left foot and left hand in front of your body, over the circle. Look into the circle. Rise on your right knee.

R2: Look over your left shoulder to see where you are going. Next, pass your left toe back and hold it at your right heel. Then slowly pass your arms close to your body until your left arm is in back and your right arm is in front.

R3: Hold this position and glide to the center.

Center: Bend your right knee, allow your right foot to glide into the new circle and push to the LBI edge, starting the new circle. Look into the new circle.

L1: Glide on the LBI edge with your left knee bent. Hold your left arm behind and your right foot and right hand in front of your body, over the circle. Look into the circle. Rise on your left knee.

L2: Look over your right shoulder to see where you are going. Next, pass your right toe back and hold it at your left heel. Then slowly pass your arms close to your body until your right arm is in back and your left arm is in front.

L3. Hold this position and glide to the center.

Repeat RBI and LBI circles, trying to trace as closely as possible.

start at center

R1

R3

center, starting circle on LBI

Sharpen Your Skills

If you hear scratching noises after you push, sit further back on the blade to avoid the toe pick. Your weight should be over the middle-front of the blade.

After the pushoff, hold the first position (R1 and L1) as strongly as possible to establish a good curve.

CHAPTER 5 FIGURES CHECKLIST

Edge exercises
__Forward outside edges
__Forward inside edges
__Back outside edges
__Back inside edges

Basic Eights
__Forward outside eight
__Forward inside eight
__Back outside eight
__Back inside eight

Chapter 6
Ice Dancing

*I*f you enjoy waltzes and tangos and other styles of dance...

If you like doing intricate steps...

If you love the combination of movement and music...

Ice dancing is the sport for you.

Ice dancing is the performance of steps set to music. It's like ballroom dancing, with the added challenges of thin blades and a slippery surface.

Ice dancing is for skaters of all ages and skill levels. It's a type of figure skating you can enjoy your entire life. Ice dancing is fun and social; you can dance solo or with a partner.

If you can skate forward edges reasonably well, you're ready to learn several of the beginning compulsory dances. When you can do three turns, mohawks and backward edges, you'll be ready to learn more complicated dances. (Review three turns, mohawks, and edges in Chapter 3: Basics.)

Many skating clubs schedule sessions on which ice dancing can be practiced. At many rinks, professional coaches offer group and private lessons for beginning ice dancers.

There are two general types of ice dances, compulsory dances and free dances.

Compulsory dances consist of required step patterns performed in time to music with a prescribed rhythm, such as waltz or tango. There are dozens of compulsory dances which are practiced by dancers all over the world. The dances are performed for recreation and also for tests and competitions.

Because the compulsory dances have prescribed steps, pattern and timing, you may attend a dance session anywhere in the United States and skate the dances with a partner. The Dutch Waltz, the first dance most skaters learn, is the same whether it's done in New York, Indiana or California.

The dances are designed to be skated by a male and female skating together, but the dances also are skated by solo skaters. Because there are more female than male dancers, most of the boys and men serve as partners for more than one girl or woman.

There are more than 30 compulsory dances in the USFSGA test structure. The dances are divided among eight levels from Preliminary through Gold and International. The ISIA program includes many of the compulsory dances in Ice Dancing Tests 2-9. On dance tests, the dancer must demonstrate for judges that he or she can perform the steps in time with the music and in unison with a partner.

A free dance is one in which a male and female couple is free to choose the steps and music. They can use known dance steps or make up movements to express an idea or a mood. Steps, turns, small lifts and small jumps are included in free dances.

"Original" dance is a type of free dance in which a couple creates their own choreography to a prescribed rhythm. Original dances are performed in upper-level competitions.

Ice dancers may take proficiency tests in free dance. The USFSA test structure includes Preliminary through Gold free dance tests. ISIA Ice Dancing Test 10 requires a free dance.

Because free dance is usually not done by beginning skaters, it is not discussed further in this book.

This chapter includes instructions for several basic dance steps, partner positions and the Dutch Waltz, one of the beginning compulsory dances.

TIPS FOR DANCERS

Here are some suggestions you should keep in mind as you learn steps and dance patterns:

1. Be aware of your posture. As you see in the photo on page 140, a dancer keeps her head and chest up, and her arms relaxed and extended to her sides.
2. Review forward stroking, page 33. When dancing, you should push by opening the skating foot (but not the hip) and using the inside edge of the blade. Do not push with the toe pick because it is an inefficient and unattractive method.
3. Always bring your feet together before taking a new step.
4. Bend the skating knee before taking a new step. Dancing on stiff legs looks and feels uncomfortable and lacks power.
5. When your free leg is extended, point your toe.

Correct erect posture and nice extension of the free leg are important in ice dancing.

BASIC STEPS

Some basic steps are found in many ice dances. On the following pages are instructions for doing the steps in the Dutch Waltz as well as some of the other steps in the other two Preliminary dances, the Canasta Tango and Rhythm Blues.

SWING ROLLS

Swing rolls can be skated forward or backward, on inside or outside edges drawing semicircles on the ice. These semicircles are also called "lobes." Instructions are provided here for forward inside and forward outside swing rolls.

You will learn to skate a series of swing rolls along an invisible line known as an axis. At first, it's best to do the rolls along an axis you can see, such as one of the hockey lines painted on the ice.

Forward swing rolls are similar to forward edges, page 119, except the free leg swings from back to front. When doing a series of swing rolls along an axis, your shoulders stay square to the axis and your hips twist under your shoulders. Square means your shoulders and arms remain perpendicular to the axis.

FORWARD OUTSIDE SWING ROLLS

In this exercise, you will skate a series of semicircles, alternating right and left outside edges, along an axis.

1. Stand with your shoulders square to the axis. Twist your hips toward your left shoulder.
2. Push to a RFO edge. Your right (skating) knee should be bent and your left (free) leg, extended behind, should be straight.
3. At the top of the semicircle, twist your hips under your shoulders and rise on your right knee. Simultaneously, pass your left leg forward close to your right foot and extend it forward in a line parallel with the skating foot. Point your left toe as your left leg swings forward.
4. As you return to the axis, bring your feet together. Twist your hips toward your right shoulder while keeping your shoulders square to the axis. Bend and stroke to the LFO edge and swing your right leg forward.
5. Repeat Steps 2 through 4, moving across the ice.

step 2

step 3

step 4

step 4

Common errors:
1. Swinging your free leg wide around your skating leg, with free toe pointed out.
2. Not pointing your free toe.
3. Not bringing your feet together before stepping to the other foot.
4. Pushing with toe picks instead of the inside edge of blade.
5. Allowing your shoulders to turn back and forth rather than keeping them square to the axis.

FORWARD INSIDE SWING ROLLS

In this exercise, you will skate a series of semicircles, alternating right and left inside edges, along an axis.

1. Stand with your shoulders square to the axis. Twist your hips toward your right shoulder.
2. Push to the RFI edge. Your right (skating) knee should be bent and your left (free) leg, extended behind, should be straight.
3. At the top of the semicircle, twist your hips under your shoulders and rise on the skating knee. Simultaneously, pass your left leg forward close to your right foot and extend it forward in a line parallel with the skating foot. Point your left toe as it passes through and extends forward. Your left leg will be bent for a short time as it passes next to the skating foot.
4. As you return to the axis, bring your feet together. Twist your hips toward your left shoulder while keeping your shoulders square to the axis. Bend and stroke to the LFI edge and swing your right leg forward.
5. Repeat Steps 2 through 4, moving across the ice.

step 3  step 2

step 4  step 4

Sharpen Your Skills — Outside or Inside Swing Rolls:

Here are some exercises you can do with inside or outside swing rolls:

Try to make each lobe (semicircle) the same size and shape. Make sure the right swing rolls, for example, aren't bigger than the left ones.

Practice swing rolls with dance music in 3/4 time that is appropriate for a waltz. Each swing roll requires a count of six: Step on beat 1, straighten the skating knee and swing the free leg forward on beat 4, return feet together on beat 6 so you are ready to step down on the next 1.

FORWARD THREE-STEP PROGRESSIVE SEQUENCE

In the Dutch Waltz and other dances, there are progressive sequences consisting of three steps. A progressive is similar to, but not the same as a crossover.

1. Glide forward on two feet counterclockwise on a circle. Turn your shoulders and arms toward the center of the circle.
2. Stroke with your right leg.
3. After pushing, your right foot strikes the ice beside and travels forward past your left foot. Push your left foot, using the outside edge of the blade, under your right leg. Extend your left leg outside the circle and trailing your right foot.
4. Lift your left foot with the blade parallel to the ice and return to the feet-together position.
5. Stroke again with your right leg. This completes a left three-step progressive sequence, which consists of a LFO edge, RFI edge and a LFO edge.
6. Repeat these steps moving clockwise around a circle to do a right three-step progressive sequence, which consists of a RFO edge, LFI edge and RFO edge.

step 3

step 3

step 2

step 5

step 4

Common errors:
1. Doing the third step of the progressive sequence on a flat or inside edge, instead of an outside edge.
2. Pushing with toe picks.

Sharpen Your Skills:

Alternate right and left progressive sequences along an axis. Bring your feet together at the end of one progressive sequence so you can push into the next progressive sequence.

Use waltz timing (counting to six) as you do each progressive: First step (beats 1, 2), second step (beat 3), third step (beats 4,5,6). Make sure the second step is quick; it's only one beat.

Bend the skating knee as deeply as possible on all three steps. Fully extend the pushing leg on each stroke and point the toes.

Note: Progressives are similar to forward crossovers (Page 36). The most important difference is in the placement of the free foot when it touches the ice.

In a progressive the free foot is placed on the ice to the outside of the skating foot, then the new skating foot progresses across the path of the old skating foot. In a crossover the free foot crosses over the skating foot before being placed on the ice.

CHASSE

A chasse is another step sequence. The second step involves a quick lift of one foot. Chasse is from a French word that means "to chase," which is what the feet do in this step sequence.

1. Glide forward on two feet counterclockwise on a circle. Turn your shoulders and arms toward the center of the circle.
2. Stroke with your right leg.
3. Bring your feet together and lift your left foot to about ankle height with the blade parallel to the ice.
4. Bring your feet back together, bend your right knee and stroke again with your right leg. This completes a left chasse sequence, consisting of a LFO edge, RFI edge while lifting the left foot, and LFO edge.
5. Repeat these steps moving clockwise on a circle to do a right chasse sequence, which consists of a RFO edge, LFI edge while lifting the right foot, and RFO edge.

step 4   step 3   step 2

Common errors:
  1. Lifting foot (on the second step) too high, too low or not parallel to the ice.
  2. Pushing with toe picks.

Sharpen Your Skills

Alternate right and left chassés along an axis. Make sure the lobes are the same size.

Count 4 beats per chassé: First step (beat 1), lift the inside foot (beat 2), third step (beats 3, 4). Use appropriate music, and do chassés with correct timing.

PARTNER POSITIONS

When dancing with a partner, it is important that both skaters maintain correct positions. Partners use their arms to create a frame in which they can move close together, without bumping into each other or tangling their feet.

Here are instructions for three partnering positions that are used in beginning dances.

KILIAN POSITION

Kilian is a side-by-side position, used when both partners are doing the same steps. The Kilian position is used in the Dutch Waltz.

1. The woman stands slightly in front and to the right of the man. Both are facing in the same direction.
2. Her left arm extends across his body to his left hand. Her left hand should be even with her waist or slightly higher. Their left hands are clasped with thumbs locked and palms lightly pressed together. His left elbow is bent and held away from his body.
3. His right arm is extended behind her back to her right hip. Her right hand presses over his right hand with her thumb tucked between his thumb and forefinger. Her right elbow is bent and held away from her body.

REVERSE KILIAN POSITION

The Reverse Kilian is the same as the Kilian position, but the woman stands to the left of the man. Her right arm extends across his body to his right hand. The Reverse Kilian position is used in the Canasta Tango, one of the Preliminary dances.

WALTZ POSITION

Waltz position is one that can be used when one partner is skating forward and the other is skating backward. Waltz position is used in the Swing Dance, one of the Pre-Bronze dances.

1. Partners stand facing each other.
2. The man's right arm reaches around to the woman's back with his hand firmly pressed against her left shoulder blade. His fingers are held together. His right elbow is slightly bent to hold her close.
3. Her left arm rests lightly on his right arm with her left hand pressed against the front of his left shoulder. Her fingers are held together.
4. His left arm and her right arm are extended to the side with a slight bend in their elbows, about as high as the woman's shoulder. Their hands are clasped with her fingers on top and palms pressed together.

DUTCH WALTZ

The Dutch Waltz is one of three dances on the USFSA Preliminary Dance Test. It is a set pattern dance, which means the steps must be performed in a specific place on the ice. The required pattern for the dance, reproduced from the USFSA *Rulebook*, is on page 153. As you read the instructions below, refer to the pattern. All of the steps are numbered.

The Dutch Waltz, according to the *Rulebook*, "is skated to slow, deliberate waltz music and consists mostly of progressive sequences and long swing rolls. Special attention should be given to the number of beats for each step in the progressive sequences in order to express the waltz rhythm of 2-1-3.

"Erect natural body position, good carriage and easy flow without too much effort are desired in the dance. The partners should strive for unison of free leg swings and for soft knee action in time with music."

Introduction:
Every compulsory dance begins with an introduction, a series of steps to gain speed and take the skater to the point on the ice where the pattern begins.

For the Dutch Waltz, a simple introduction consists of four steps across the short end of the rink. Many skaters start on the red dot in the middle of a hockey circle. See the diagram for the introduction on page 153.

Intro Step 1: Left (3 beats)
Intro Step 2: Right (3 beats)
Intro Step 3: Left (3 beats)
Intro Step 4: Right (3 beats)

Side pattern:
The first section of the dance is a sequence of four lobes (or semicircles) along an axis. Each lobe starts and ends on the axis.

Steps 1,2,3: The first lobe is a three-step left progressive sequence: Left outside edge (2 beats), right inside edge (1 beat), left outside edge (3 beats). Bring your feet together on beat 6.

Step 4. Bend and stroke to your right foot for a RFO swing roll (6 beats). Bring your feet together.

Step 5. Bend and stroke to your left foot for a LFO swing roll (6 beats). Bring your feet together.

Step 6,7,8: Bend and stroke to a right three-step progressive sequence: right outside edge (2 beats), left inside edge (1 beat), right outside edge (3 beats). Bring your feet together.

End pattern:
The pattern across the short end of the rink begins and ends with a two-step corner sequence: LFO edge, RFI edge. (Steps 9 and 10, and Steps 15 and 16.)

Step 9: Left outside edge (3 beats). Bring your feet together.
Step 10: Right inside edge on the same lobe (3 beats).
Steps 11, 12, 13: On the same lobe going around the corner, do a three-step left progressive sequence: left outside edge (2 beats), right inside edge (1 beat), left outside edge (3 beats). Bring your feet together.
Step 14: Bend and stroke to your right foot for a RFO swing roll (6 beats). Bring your feet together.
Step 15: The first of two corner steps: left outside edge (3 beats). Bring your feet together.
Step 16: Second corner step: right inside edge on the same lobe (3 beats).

This completes one pattern of the Dutch Waltz. Without stopping, you can start another pattern, starting with Steps 1,2,3, the left progressive sequence. Do not repeat the introduction between patterns. It takes two patterns to make one complete circuit around the ice surface. If you go around the arena several times doing the Dutch Waltz, you should try to trace your pattern on the ice.

Doing the Dutch Waltz with a partner:
The Dutch Waltz is done in Kilian position: The woman stands to the right of the man.

The shoulders of both partners should stay in the same line, while their hips twist under their shoulders. This alignment will make it easier for the partners to stay together on the lobes and when making transitions from lobe to lobe.

The person skating on the outside of the lobe should be slightly in front. At the end of the lobe, the other person takes a slight lead. This is called tracking.

Sharpen Your Skills:
Practice patterns of the Dutch Waltz without music until you can remember the steps.

Practice the patterns while counting in waltz time, making sure the progressive sequences are counted 2-1-3 and the swing rolls take six beats.

Then do the Dutch Waltz with music. The specifications for the music are 3/4 time, 46 measures of 3 beats, 138 beats per minute. Appropriate music likely will be played during dance sessions at your rink.

When you can do the Dutch Waltz solo, try it with a partner.

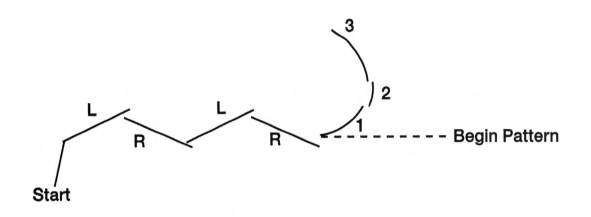

The introduction to the Dutch Waltz consists of four forward strokes — left, right, left, right.

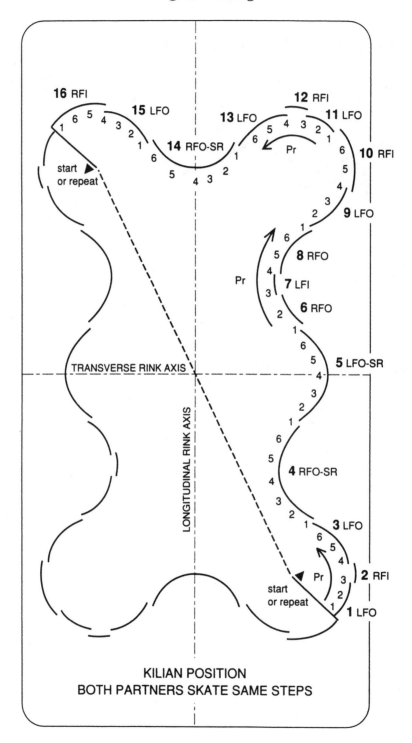

16 RFI
15 LFO
13 LFO
12 RFI
11 LFO
14 RFO-SR
10 RFI
Pr
start or repeat
9 LFO
8 RFO
Pr
7 LFI
6 RFO
5 LFO-SR
TRANSVERSE RINK AXIS
LONGITUDINAL RINK AXIS
4 RFO-SR
3 LFO
2 RFI
start or repeat
Pr
1 LFO

KILIAN POSITION
BOTH PARTNERS SKATE SAME STEPS

CHAPTER 6: ICE DANCING CHECKLIST

The first step to becoming an ice dancer to is master the skills on this list. The skills are listed in order of difficulty. When you have mastered one skill, check it off, and move on to the next skill on the list.

Basic Steps:
    __Forward outside swing roll
    __Forward inside swing roll
    __3-step progressive sequence*
    __Chassé

Partner Positions:
    __Kilian position*
    __Reverse Kilian position
    __Waltz position

Dutch Waltz
    __Side Pattern
    __End Pattern

    * Element of the Dutch Waltz.